Praise for *The Art of Possibility*

"The passionate energy permeating *The Art of Possibility* is a true force for every reader for self-development and life fulfillment."

—KLAUS SCHWAB,
    Founder and President, World Economic Forum

"*The Art of Possibility* makes a humane and brilliant future possible. I truly want everyone to read this book—it opens us to the treasure of our great human capacity for creativity. These practices are simple yet extraordinarily effective for tapping into the unlimited energy of the human imagination."

—MARGARET J. WHEATLEY,
    Author of *Leadership and the New Science*, Coauthor of
    A Simpler Way, and President, The Berkana Institute

"I love this book. It is provocative, instructive, and uplifting. The ideas and practices in it are about creating and engaging new possibilities in life. It is a boon to readers as a guide to their personal development, as well as a resource for helping them to lead others. *The Art of Possibility* is a gem."

—PETER J. FROST, Edgar F. Kaiser Chair of
    Organizational Behavior, University of British Columbia

"For one relatively brief period in the history of philosophy, namely, the Hellenistic age, philosophers saw their job as a practical one: they wanted to help people think about their lives and the world in a way that would make them happier and more fulfilled. The Zanders are clear about the fact that they are offering tools rather than answers, and stimulation rather than comfort. But their project has much in common with that now almost abandoned therapeutic strain in philosophy, and no shortage of new ideas."

—ANTHONY GOTTLIEB, Author of *The Dream of Reason:*
    A History of Philosophy from the Greeks to the Renaissance, and
    Executive Editor, *The Economist*

"This elegantly written book presents a series of practices that begin with acceptance and harmony rather than strategy and maneuvering. *The Art of Possibility* is also a chronicle of a unique life partnership, told in colorful parables. Ben and Roz Zander are innovators, and they are generous with their secrets. All musicians learn that they must do more than survive defeats and rejections—they must transform them. The Zanders open bright new avenues, leading us into a less driven, more habitable world lit by humor, patience, and compassion."

—JOHN HARBISON, Pulitzer Prize–winning Composer

"Reading *The Art of Possibility* is like completing a series of music lessons for the soul. Readers will recognize not only that they can create wholly new life forms for themselves, but that these forms actually alter the audiences for whom they play. And the great thing is, no one is tone deaf. *The Art of Possibility* has captured me, and I embrace it!"

—THOMAS J. COTTLE,
   Psychologist and Professor of Education, Boston University

"This is a wise, uplifting, and important work, a seamless blend of insight and inspiration, personal revelations, and stories drawn from the worlds of art, psychology, business, and politics. Ben and Roz Zander make an extraordinary team—their energy, passion, and fundamental commitment to humane values are absolutely contagious."

—DORIS KEARNS GOODWIN, Historian and
   Pulitzer Prize–winning Author of *No Ordinary Time: Franklin and Eleanor Roosevelt: The Home Front in World War II*

A BOOK OF PRACTICES

The
Possi

THE
Art of Possibility

Rosamund
Stone
Zander

Benjamin
Zander

PENGUIN BOOKS

PENGUIN BOOKS

Published by the Penguin Group

Penguin Group (USA) Inc., 375 Hudson Street, New York, New York 10014, U.S.A.

Penguin Group (Canada), 90 Eglinton Avenue East, Suite 700, Toronto,
   Ontario, Canada M4P 2Y3 (a division of Pearson Penguin Canada Inc.)

Penguin Books Ltd, 80 Strand, London WC2R 0RL, England

Penguin Ireland, 25 St Stephen's Green, Dublin 2, Ireland (a division of Penguin Books Ltd)

Penguin Group (Australia), 250 Camberwell Road, Camberwell,
   Victoria 3124, Australia (a division of Pearson Australia Group Pty Ltd)

Penguin Books India Pvt Ltd, 11 Community Centre, Panchsheel Park, New Delhi – 110 017, India

Penguin Group (NZ), cnr Airborne and Rosedale Roads,
   Albany, Auckland 1310, New Zealand (a division of Pearson New Zealand Ltd)

Penguin Books (South Africa) (Pty) Ltd, 24 Sturdee Avenue,
   Rosebank, Johannesburg 2196, South Africa

Penguin Books Ltd, Registered Offices: 80 Strand, London WC2R 0RL, England

First published in the United States of America by Harvard Business School Press 2000
Published in Penguin Books 2002

54 53 52 51 50

Some of the names of real individuals have been disguised to protect their confidentiality
or privacy. In all other cases, real names have been used with authorization.

"I Dwell in Possibility" by Emily Dickinson is reprinted by permission of the publishers and
the trustees of Amherst College, from *The Poems of Emily Dickinson*, Thomas H. Johnson,
editor, Cambridge, Mass.: The Belknap Press of Harvard University Press, copyright © 1951,
1955, 1979 by the President and Fellows of Harvard College.

Quotation from Dr. Martin Luther King, Jr., is reprinted by arrangement with The Heirs to
the Estate of Martin Luther King, Jr., c/o Writers House, Inc., as agent for the proprietor.
Copyright 1963 by Martin Luther King, Jr., copyright renewed 1991 by Coretta Scott King.

Quotation from the movie *Babe* is from *Babe*, directed by Chris Noonan, produced by
George Miller, Doug Mitchell, and Bill Miller. Copyright © 1995 Universal City Studios Inc.

Quotation from the movie *The Shawshank Redemption* is from *The Shawshank Redemption*, directed by Frank Darabont, produced by Niki Marvin. Copyright © 1994 Castle Rock
Entertainment.

THE LIBRARY OF CONGRESS HAS CATALOGED THE HARDCOVER EDITION AS FOLLOWS:
Zander, Rosamund Stone, 1942–
The art of possibility / Rosamund Stone Zander, Benjamin Zander.
p.   cm.
ISBN 0-87584-770-6 (hc.)
ISBN 0 14 20.0110 4 (pbk.)
1. Possibility. I. Zander, Benjamin, 1939– II. Title.
BC199.P7 Z36 2000
153.7—dc21   00-033537

Printed in the United States of America

I dwell in Possibility—
A fairer House than Prose—
More numerous of Windows—
Superior—for Doors—

Of Chambers as the Cedars—
Impregnable of Eye—
And for an Everlasting Roof—
The Gambrels of the Sky—

Of Visitors—the fairest—
For Occupation—This—
The spreading wide my narrow Hands—
To gather Paradise—

—EMILY DICKINSON

Contents

An Invitation to Possibility

BEN: "Waiter," I said, in an exuberant mood, "I have a perfect life, but I don't have a knife."

I was having breakfast with a friend on one of my periodic visits to London to conduct the Philharmonia Orchestra. I heard giggles behind me and, turning around, caught the eye of a girl of about twelve with a typically English pudding-bowl haircut. We exchanged smiles, and then I went back to my conversation and to my breakfast.

The next day, I passed the young lady again in the breakfast room and stopped to speak with her.

"Good morning. How are you today?"

She drew herself up ever so slightly and, with a tilt to her chin and a sparkle in her eye, answered me.

"Perfect," she said.

Later, when she was leaving with her parents, I called out mischievously, "Have a perfect day!"

"I will!" she responded, as though it were the easiest, most obvious choice in the world.

And with that, she sailed out into a universe of possibility.

Launching the Journey

THIS IS A HOW-TO BOOK of an unusual kind. Unlike the genre of how-to books that offer strategies to surmount the hurdles of a competitive world and move out ahead, the objective of this book is to provide the reader the means to lift off from that world of struggle and sail into a vast universe of possibility. Our premise is that many of the circumstances that seem to block us in our daily lives may only appear to do so based on a framework of assumptions we carry with us. Draw a different frame around the same set of circumstances and new pathways come into view. Find the right framework and extraordinary accomplishment becomes an everyday experience. Each chapter of this book presents a different facet of this approach and describes a new practice for bringing possibility to life.

THE PARTNERSHIP

We, the authors, Ben and Roz, have developed this outlook from two different, though mutually enhancing, perspectives. Ben is the conductor of the Boston Philharmonic Orchestra, a teacher and a communicator of rare ability who engages passionately with orchestras, audiences, and the public at large. He has unbounded energy to entice people to accomplish the extraordinary and to see each venture through. He finds the tempo in music, in speaking, and in action that throws us into motion. If there is a tempo of transformation, Ben moves on its pulse. To help us all along, he plays persuasively on our minds and heartstrings through story-telling, humor, and music. His is the exuberant public voice of this partnership.

Roz functions in an intimate arena. She has a private practice in family therapy, runs accomplishment groups, and works with people in many settings to transform issues and conflicts. She pays close attention to the stories people tell about who they are and how their world works, and she gives them tools to rename them-selves and their circumstances in a way that generally leads to an outcome that is more than they hoped for or even imagined. She listens for the desire in people for something new, for conditions that do not exist, and she helps them create a framework that would make these conditions possible. Roz practices the art of pos-sibility also from the perspective of a landscape painter and writer. In this book, she frames the issues, while the stories pass from voice to voice.

Together, we work as a team. Ben's public presence often brings him face to face with challenging situations that call for new kinds of leadership and new conceptual frameworks. When the questions he brings to Roz appear to have broad application, she goes to the drawing board to sketch out an approach. He then takes the new designs into the public arena to try them out. This is the essence of our enlivening, constantly moving partnership. Our joint conviction is that much, much more is possible than people ordinarily think.

THE DESIGN

The initial offer from the Harvard Business School Press that we write this book for a business as well as a lay audience was a rare opportunity, and one that has not often been available to people working in the arts. Historically, artists have been employed by leading institutions to bring emotional truth to established principles. Yet in our new global society, no institution has the wide acceptance to create values and direction for the majority of people. Markets in free societies are rapidly replacing governments and religious institutions as regulators of the highest authority, and markets perform without values; they do not converse in a human tongue. The arts can break new ground here, bringing human consciousness to bear on these flows of product and capital, energizing our interpersonal connections, and opening new doors for invention and practice.

Revolutionary shifts in the operational structures of our world seem to call for new definitions of who we are and what we are here for. That a vote taken in Europe, a financial decision made in Tokyo, or an unusually warm flow in the South Pacific can directly affect lives a world apart calls into question our assumption that we are self-activated and self-managed. Our customary mind-set about who we are may even undermine our ability to have a say in the way things go from here. So this is a book with suggestions for novel ways of defining ourselves, others, and the world we live in—ways that may be more apt for the challenges of our time. It uses the metaphor of music, and relies on all the arts. Art, after all, is about *rearranging* us, creating surprising juxtapositions, emotional openings, startling presences, flight paths to the eternal.

THE VISION

Like a piece of music, this book has a long song line, a theme upon which each chapter is a variation. The long line portrays a world where the conflict between the individual and the collective that is intrinsic to our everyday reality resolves. In this vision, an individual's unique expression plays an integral and constructive part in setting a direction for the group—in fact, for all of humankind. The long line is the possibility of seeing deeply into what is best for all of us, seeing the next step. Each chapter of the book offers a separate practice for realizing that vision. Each practice provides an opportunity for personal evolution that promises to enhance not only the reader's life but also the organizations and relationships in which he or she participates. These practices are as relevant to corporate management as they are to a marriage; as relevant to acts of diplomacy as to the settlement of family disputes.

PRACTICES

Standard social and business practices are built on certain assumptions—shared understandings that have evolved from older beliefs and conditions. And while circumstances may have changed since the start of these practices, their continued use tends to reconfirm the old beliefs. For this reason our daily practices feel right and true to us, regardless of whether they have evolved to keep up with the pace of change. In just such a way a business culture arises and perpetuates itself, perhaps long after its usefulness has passed.

This book offers practices that are transformational—practices that may "feel" illogical or counterintuitive to our normal understanding of how things operate. Their purpose is to initiate a new approach to current conditions, based on uncommon assumptions about the nature of the world. The history of transformational phenomena—the Internet, for example, or paradigm shifts in science, or the spread of a new religion—suggests that transformation happens less by arguing cogently for something new than by generating active, ongoing practices that shift a culture's experience of the basis for reality.

So the practices presented in this book are not about making incremental changes that lead to new ways of doing things based on old beliefs, and they are not about self-improvement. They are geared instead toward causing a total shift of posture, perceptions, beliefs, and thought processes. They are about transforming your entire world.

Notes on Practicing

BEN: Although the practices we offer here are simple, they are not easy. I am reminded of a dispiriting moment in a cello lesson with my teacher, Mr. Herbert Withers. He was eighty-three years old, and I was eleven. I had tried to play a passage, but I couldn't make it work. I tried again, and it didn't work, and a third time, and I was no more successful. I remember making a frustrated grimace and putting down my bow. The elderly Mr.Withers leaned over me and whispered, "What? You've been practicing it for three minutes, and you *still* can't play it?"

Our practices will take a good deal more than three minutes to master. Additionally, everything you think and feel and see around you will argue against them. So it takes dedication, a leap of faith, and, yes, *practicing* to get them into your repertoire.

ROZ: A dozen summers ago, I signed up for my first white-water rafting trip, on Maine's Kennebec River. Traveling overland in a rickety bus to reach the launch point, I paid close attention to the guide standing in the aisle, as she undertook our education about this popular sport.

"If you fall out of the boat," she said, "it is very important that you pull your feet up so that you don't get a foot caught in the rocks below. Think *toes to nose*," she stressed, and gave us a precarious demonstration, bracing herself and hoisting one foot toward her nose, "*then look for the boat and reach for the oar or the rope.*"

Our guide chattered on as we bumped our way toward the river. Most of us had been on the road since 4 A.M. and were feeling sleepy and mesmerized by the vibrations of the bus. "*Toes to nose,*" I heard again. And then, "*look for the boat.*"

By the time we arrived at the river's edge, I had heard the two phrases so many times I felt slightly crazed. We put on our wet suits, gathered our equipment, and stood in a circle for our final instructions.

"If you fall out of the boat what do you say to yourself?"

"Toes to nose and look for the boat," we chimed.

Someone here is mentally challenged, I thought, as we climbed into the boat and started downstream.

Surging into the only class 5 rapids of the journey, I vanished into a wall of water that rose up at the stern of the raft, as into a black hole. Roiling about underwater, there was no up and down, neither water nor air nor land. There had never been a boat. There was no anywhere, there was nothing at all.

Toes to nose . . . the words emerged from a void. I pulled together into a ball. Air. Sounds. *Look for the boat* . . . did that come from my head or was someone calling? The boat appeared, and an oar. *Reach for the oar* . . . I did, and found myself in a world, inside the boat, on the water, traveling down the Kennebec in a spew of foam.

Since this experience, I have used the metaphor "out of the boat" with many people in different situations. It signifies more than being off track—it means you don't know where the track is anymore. "Out of the boat" could refer to something as simple as losing all memory of ever having been on an exercise program, or it could refer to floundering in the wake of a management shake-up. When you are out of the boat, you cannot *think* your way back in; you have no point of reference. You must call on something that has been established in advance, a catch phrase, like *"toes to nose."*

In the chapters that follow, you will be introduced to a set of practices that each has its own catchphrase, such as *it's all invented,* or *giving an A,* or *Rule Number 6.* By the time you have read the stories, parables, and first-person accounts that illuminate each of these practices, you will be better able to recall them with the use of the catch phrases, just as I was able to get back in the boat by remembering *toes to nose.* Once you are in the habit of using them, these practices will reliably land you back in the boat, reoriented in a universe of possibility.

Now, on to the river . . .

PRACTICES IN POSSIBILITY

It's All

Invented

A shoe factory sends two marketing scouts to a region of Africa to study the prospects for expanding business. One sends back a telegram saying,

SITUATION HOPELESS STOP NO ONE WEARS SHOES

The other writes back triumphantly,

GLORIOUS BUSINESS OPPORTUNITY STOP THEY HAVE NO SHOES

To THE MARKETING EXPERT who sees no shoes, all the evidence points to hopelessness. To his colleague, the same conditions point to abundance and possibility. Each scout comes to the scene with his own perspective; each returns telling a different tale. Indeed, all of life comes to us in narrative form; it's a story we tell.

The roots of this phenomenon go much deeper than just attitude or personality. Experiments in neuroscience have demonstrated that we reach an understanding of the world in roughly this sequence: first, our senses bring us selective information about what is out there; second, the brain constructs its own simulation of the sensations; and only then, third, do we have our first conscious experience of our milieu. The world comes into our consciousness in the form of a map already drawn, a story already told, a hypothesis, a construction of our own making.

A now-classic 1953 experiment revealed to stunned researchers that a frog's eye is capable of perceiving only four types of phenomena[1]:

- Clear lines of contrast
- Sudden changes in illumination
- Outlines in motion
- Curves of outlines of small, dark objects

A frog does not "see" its mother's face, it cannot appreciate a sunset, nor even the nuances of color. It "sees" only what it needs to see in order to eat and to avoid being eaten: small tasty bugs, or the sudden movement of a stork coming in its direction. The frog's eye delivers extremely selective information to the frog's brain. The frog perceives only that which fits into its hardwired categories of perception.

Human eyes are selective, too, though magnitudes more complex than those of the frog. We think we can see "everything," until we remember that bees make out patterns written in ultraviolet light on flowers, and owls see in the dark. The senses of every species are fine-tuned to perceive information critical to their survival—dogs hear sounds above our range of hearing, insects pick up molecular traces emitted from potential mates acres away.

We *perceive* only the sensations we are programmed to receive, and our awareness is further restricted by the fact that we *recognize* only those for which we have mental maps or categories.

The British neuropsychologist Richard Gregory wrote, "The senses do not give us a picture of the world directly; rather they provide evidence for the checking of hypotheses about what lies

---

[1] J. Y. Lettvin, H. R. Maturana, W. S. McCulloch, and W. H. Pitts, "What the Frog's Eye Tells the Frog's Brain," *Proceedings of the IRE* 47 (1940–1951), 1959, cited by Tor Nørretranders, *The User Illusion*, trans. Jonathan Syndenham (New York: Viking Penguin, 1991), 192–193.

before us."[2] And neurophysiologist Donald O. Hebb says, "The 'real world' is a construct, and some of the peculiarities of scientific thought become more intelligible when this fact is recognized . . . Einstein himself in 1926 told Heisenberg it was nonsense to found a theory on observable facts alone: 'In reality the very opposite happens. It is theory which decides what we can observe.'"[3]

We see a map of the world, not the world itself. But what kind of map is the brain inclined to draw? The answer comes from one of the realities of biology, the survival of the fittest. Fundamentally, it is a map that has to do with our very survival; it is designed to provide, as a first priority, information on immediate dangers to life and limb, the ability to distinguish friends and foes, the wherewithal to find food and resources and opportunities for procreation. The world appears to us sorted and packaged in this way, substantially enriched by the categories of culture we live in, by learning, and by the meanings we form out of the unique journey each of us travels.

See how thoroughly the map and its categories govern our perception. In a famous experiment, the Me'en people of Ethiopia were presented for the first time with photographs of people and animals, but were unable to "read" the two-dimensional image. "They felt the paper, sniffed it, crumpled it, and listened to the crackling noise it made; they nipped off little bits and chewed them to taste it."[4] Yet people in our modern world easily equate the photographic image with the object photographed—even though the two resemble each other only in a very abstract sense. Recognizing Pablo Picasso in a train compartment, a man inquired of the artist why he did not paint people "the way they really are." Picasso asked what he meant by that expression. The man opened his wallet and took out a snapshot of his wife, saying, "That's my wife." Picasso responded, "Isn't she rather small and flat?"[5]

---

[2] Richard L. Gregory, *Eye and Brain: The Psychology of Seeing*, 4th ed. (Princeton University Press, 1990), 21–22, cited by Nørretranders, *The User Illusion*, 186.

[3] D. O. Hebb, "Science and the World of Imagination," *Canadian Psychology* 16 (1975), 4–11.

[4] J. B. Deregowski, "Real Space and Represented Space: Cross-Cultural Perspectives," *The Behavioral and Brain Sciences* 12 (1989), 57, cited by Nørretranders, *The User Illusion*, 187.

[5] Heinz R. Pagels, *The Dreams of Reason* (New York: Bantam, 1988), 163, cited by Nørretranders, *The User Illusion*, 188.

For the Me'en people there were no "photographs," although they lay in their hands as plain as day. They saw nothing but shiny paper. Only through the conventions of modern life do we see the image in a photograph. As for Picasso, he was able to see the snapshot as an artifact, distinct from what it represented.

Our minds are also designed to string events into story lines, whether or not there is any connection between the parts. In dreams, we regularly weave sensations gathered from disparate parts of our lives into narratives. In full wakefulness, we produce reasons for our actions that are rational, plausible, and guided by the logic of cause and effect, whether or not these "reasons" accurately portray any of the real motivational forces at work. Experiments with people who have suffered a lesion between the two halves of the brain have shown that when the right side is prompted, say, to close a door, the left side, unaware of the experimenter's instruction, will produce a "reason" as to why he has just performed the action, such as, "Oh, I felt a draft."[6]

It is these sorts of phenomena that we are referring to when we use the catchphrase for this chapter *it's all invented*. What we mean is, "It's all invented anyway, so we might as well invent a story or a framework of meaning that enhances our quality of life and the life of those around us."

Most people already understand that, as with cultural differences, interpretations of the world vary from individual to individual and from group to group. This understanding may persuade us that by factoring out our own interpretations of reality, we can reach a solid truth. However, the term *it's all invented* points to a more fundamental notion—that no matter how objective we try to be, it is still through the structure of the brain that we perceive the world. So, if there are absolutes, we have no direct access to their existence. The mind *constructs*. The meanings our minds construct may be widely shared and sustaining for us, but they may have little to do with the world itself. Furthermore, how would we know?

Even science—which is often too simply described as an

---

[6] Michael Gazzaniga, *The Social Brain* (New York: Basic Books, 1985), 70–72 .

orderly process of accumulating knowledge based on previously acquired truths—even *science* relies on our capacity to adapt to new facts by radically shifting the theoretical constructions we previously accepted as truth. When we lived in a Newtonian world, we saw straight lines and forces; in an Einsteinian universe, we noticed curved space/time, relativity, and indeterminacy. The Newtonian view is still as valid—only now we see it as a special case, valid within a particular set of conditions. Each new paradigm gives us the opportunity to "see" phenomena that were before as invisible to us as the colors of the sunset to the frog.

To gain greater insight into what we mean by a map, a framework, or a paradigm, let's revisit the famous nine-dot puzzle, which will be familiar to many readers. As you may or may not know, the puzzle asks us to *join all nine dots with four straight lines, without taking pen from paper.* If you have never seen this puzzle before, go ahead and try it . . . before you turn the page!

• • •

• • •

• • •

If you have never played this game before, you will most likely find yourself struggling to solve the puzzle inside the space of the dots, as though the outer dots constituted the outer limit of the puzzle. The puzzle illustrates a universal phenomenon of the human mind, the necessity to sort data into categories in order to perceive it. Your brain instantly classifies the nine dots as a two-dimensional square. And there they rest, like nails in the coffin of any further possibility, establishing a box with a dot in each of the four corners, even though no box in fact exists on the page.

Nearly everybody adds that context to the instructions, nearly everybody *hears:* "Connect the dots with four straight lines without taking pen from paper, *within the square formed by the outer dots.*" And within that framework, there is no solution. If, however, we were to amend the original set of instructions by adding the phase, *"Feel free to use the whole sheet of paper,"* it is likely that a new possibility would suddenly appear to you.

It might seem that the space outside the dots was crying out, *"Hey, bring some lines out here!"*

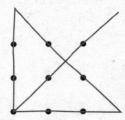

The frames our minds create define—and *confine*—what we perceive to be possible. Every problem, every dilemma, every dead end we find ourselves facing in life, only appears unsolvable inside a particular frame or point of view. Enlarge the box, or create another frame around the data, and problems vanish, while new opportunities appear.

This practice we refer to by the catchphrase, *it's all invented,* is the most fundamental of all the practices we present in this book. When you bring to mind *it's all invented,* you remember that it's all a story you tell—not just some of it, but all of it. And remember, too, that every story you tell is founded on a network of hidden assumptions. If you learn to notice and distinguish these stories, you will be able to break through the barriers of any "box" that contains unwanted conditions and create other conditions or narratives that support the life you envision for yourself and those around you. We do not mean that you can just make anything up and have it magically appear. We mean that you can shift the framework to one whose underlying assumptions allow for the conditions you desire. Let your thoughts and actions spring from the new framework and see what happens.

THE PRACTICE

A simple way to practice *it's all invented* is to ask yourself this question:

> *What assumption am I making,*
> *That I'm not aware I'm making,*
> *That gives me what I see?*

And when you have an answer to that question, ask yourself this one:

> *What might I now invent,*
> *That I haven't yet invented,*
> *That would give me other choices?*

And then you can invent spaces, like the paper surrounding the nine dots, where four lines can do the work of five.

We now move on to the second practice, which entails inventing a new universe to live in, a universe of possibility.

STEPPING INTO A
Universe of

Possibility

ONCE YOU HAVE BEGUN to distinguish that *it's all invented*, you can create a place to dwell where new inventions are the order of the day. Such a place we call "the universe of possibility," and stepping into it is our second practice. This universe—like the page that holds the nine dots—extends beyond the borders that confine us to our everyday reality.

You may ask, "What are these borders, and what is this everyday reality?"

THE WORLD OF MEASUREMENT

We propose to call our familiar everyday world the "world of measurement" in order to highlight the central position held by assessments, scales, standards, grades, and comparisons. In this story of the everyday, each of us strives for success, hoping to arrive at a better place than where we are. On our path to achieving a goal we inevitably encounter obstacles. Some of the more familiar ones, aside from other people, are scarcities of time, money, power, love, resources, and inner strength.

All the manifestations of the world of measurement—the winning and losing, the gaining of acceptance and the threatened rejection, the raised hopes and the dash into despair—all are based on a single assumption that is hidden from our awareness. The assumption is that life is about staying alive and making it through—*surviving* in a world of scarcity and peril. Even when life is at its best in the measurement world, this assumption is the backdrop for the play, and, like the invisible box around the nine dots, it keeps the universe of possibility out of view.

Certain responses are better suited than others to an environment where survival is the issue, all of which are prevalent in the world of measurement. Alertness to danger, a clever strategic mind, an eye for assessing friend and foe, a knack for judging strength and weakness, the know-how to take possession of resources, a measure of mistrust, and a good dollop of fear are some of the qualities that will safeguard us. Keeping our armor intact is of critical importance as well, which means resisting any challenge to our personal viewpoint.

We also feel more secure when we can identify objects and determine their location. An indication of this is that the term *mine*field stands as a universally appreciated metaphor for danger. It feels safer to deal with reality as though it were fixed, as though people, ideas, and situations can be fully known and measured.

We grow up in a world of measurement, and in this world, we get to know each other and things by measuring them, and by comparing and contrasting them. We know a child as compared to other children, a performance of a Puccini aria by a local tenor as contrasted to one sung by Pavarotti, or a company's year-end statement as it stacks up to earlier projections. In order to be in a position to assess, judge, and report on circumstances, the individual stands back, identifying himself, and by extension his group, as separate from others. That opinionated "little voice in the head" is almost always speaking from Measurement Central. Life in the measurement world seems to be arranged in hierarchies: some groups, people, bodies, places, and ideas seem better or more powerful than others. Lines appear, dividing an inside from an outside: some people, races, and organizations are safer and more desirable to belong to than others. There are only so many pieces of the pie.

The dramatic action in this world of success and failure has to do with overcoming odds and prevailing, or being acknowledged and included. Virtually every children's book, every made-for-television special follows the pattern. Competition is the vehicle to success, and metaphors based on competitive sports and war are applied to almost any situation. Conversations among friends chronicle personal trials and triumphs. Certain feelings mirror the ups and downs of fortune in the world of measurement: love for our own, for instance, and sympathy for those weaker than we are; fear, anger, and despair at losing; and, of course, the exhilaration of having come out on top.

Just as virtually everybody adds the clause *within the square formed by the outer dots* to the instructions for the nine-dot puzzle; virtually everybody, whether living in the lap of luxury or in diminished circumstances, wakes up in the morning with the unseen assumption that life is about the struggle to survive and get ahead in a world of limited resources.

"Hey, bring some lines out here!"

A UNIVERSE OF POSSIBILITY

Let us suppose, now, that a universe of possibility stretches beyond the world of measurement to include all worlds: infinite, generative, and abundant. Unimpeded on a daily basis by the concern for survival, free from the generalized assumption of scarcity, a person stands in the great space of possibility in a posture of openness, with an unfettered imagination for what can be.

In the realm of possibility, we gain our knowledge by invention. We decide that the essence of a child is joy, and joy she is. Our small business attracts the label, "The Can-Do Company," and that is exactly who we are. We speak with the awareness that language creates categories of meaning that open up new worlds to explore. Life appears as variety, pattern, and shimmering movement, inviting us in every moment to engage. The pie is enormous, and if you take a slice, the pie is whole again.

The action in a universe of possibility may be characterized as generative, or giving, in all senses of that word—producing new life, creating new ideas, consciously endowing with meaning, contributing, yielding to the power of contexts. The relationship *between* people and environments is highlighted, not the people and things themselves. Emotions that are often relegated to the special category of spirituality are abundant here: joy, grace, awe, wholeness, passion, and compassion.

There are moments in everyone's life when an experience of integration with the world transcends the business of survival— like seeing a grandchild for the first time, witnessing an Olympic record broken or the uncommon bravery of an ordinary citizen. For many, the experience of attending the dismantling of the Berlin Wall or of witnessing the emergence of Nelson Mandela from twenty-seven years of imprisonment may have been such a moment. Some find admission to the realm of possibility at a religious gathering, some in meditation, some by listening to great music. Often people enter this state in the presence of natural beauty or at the sight of something of infinite magnitude, an expanse of ocean or a towering sky. These are moments when we forget our*selves* and seem to become part of all being.

DOWN TO EARTH IN A UNIVERSE OF POSSIBILITY

It may seem that this chapter sets up a simplistic dichotomy between being successful and living a kind-hearted, feel-good life.

Nothing could be further from our conviction. In fact, we are saying that, *on the whole*, you are more likely to extend your business *and* have a fulfilled life if you have the attitude that there are always new customers out there waiting to be enrolled rather than that money, customers, and ideas are in short supply. You are more likely to be successful, *overall*, if you participate joyfully with projects and goals and do not think your life depends on achieving the mark because then you will be better able to connect to people all around you. On the whole, resources are likely to come to you in greater abundance when you are generous and inclusive and engage people in your passion for life. There aren't any guarantees, of course. When you are oriented to abundance, you care less about being in control, and you take more risks. You may give away short-term profits in pursuit of a bigger dream; you may take a long view without being able to predict the outcome. In the measurement world, you set a goal and strive for it. In the universe of possibility, you set the context and let life unfold.

SURVIVAL AND SURVIVAL-THINKING

Many people's lives are in daily jeopardy, and they must and do concentrate on staying alive, as any one of us would if held up on the street or lost at sea. That is not the same as survival-*thinking*, which is the undiscriminating, ongoing attitude that life is dangerous and that one must put one's energy into looking out for Number One.

True scarcity and scarcity-*thinking* are different phenomena as well. There are regions of the world where resources are locally scarce, where people lack for their most fundamental needs. However, scarcity-*thinking* is an attitude as prevalent among the well-heeled as among the down-at-heel, and remains unaltered by a change in circumstances. It is a fatalistic outlook, as profiled by the English economist Thomas Malthus in his 1798 "Essay on the Principle of Population" that predicts that supplies—which appear fixed and limited—will eventually run out. This attitude prompts us to seek to acquire more for ourselves no matter how much we have and to treat others as competitors no matter how little they have. Scarcity-thinking and real scarcity are interactive in the simple sense that the frenzied accumulation of resources by some leaves others without enough, in a world that has the means to supply the basic needs of everyone. They are correlated in that the indiscriminate use of the earth's resources, at a rate faster than the earth can regenerate, leaves the next generation with shrinking reserves.

How to Step There

Now we come to the heart of the matter. What is the practice that orients you to a universe of possibility? It is a practice for revealing the hidden framework from which the world of measurement springs. When you see how thoroughly that framework, like the box around the nine dots, rules your life, you will have located yourself in the realm of possibility beyond it. So, first, ask yourself:

> *How are my thoughts and actions, in this moment, reflections of the measurement world?*

You look for thoughts and actions that reflect survival and scarcity, comparison and competition, attachment and anxiety. Notice that the question is not, "*Are* my thoughts . . ." which is a question of assessment, but, "*How* are my thoughts . . ." which is a true inquiry. See how easy it is to argue that you are an exception, that you personally are not governed by any such set of assumptions. This, of course, is another example of the measurement world at work.

So when you notice yourself thinking, for instance, that this line of inquiry must apply to men more than to women because men are so competitive, and you recognize *that* thought as your first bit of evidence that your measurement mind is at work, you ask yourself again:

> *How are my thoughts and actions, in this new moment, a reflection of the measurement world?*
>
> *And how now?*

You keep asking the question until you finally appreciate how hopeless it is to escape being shaped by the assumptions that underlie all of life. And then you may begin to laugh. And when someone asks, "How are you?" it may appear to you utterly ridiculous to try to assess yourself, or to express life as a struggle and a burden, and before you know it, the word "perfect" may just pop out. And you will be smiling. For you will have stepped into a universe of possibility.

Of course, you won't have *arrived*.

Giving

an A

AT THE UNIVERSITY OF Southern California, a leadership course was taught each year to fifty of the most outstanding students out of twenty-seven thousand in the school, hand-picked by each department. At the end of the semester, the grader for the course was instructed to give one-third of the students A's, one-third B's and one-third C's—even though the work of any member of this class was likely to surpass that of any other student in the university. Imagine the blow to the morale of the eager and hard-working student who received the requisite C.

Not just in this case, but in most cases, grades say little about the work done. When you reflect to a student that he has misconstrued a concept or has taken a false step in a math problem, you are indicating something real about his performance, but when you give him a B+, you are saying nothing at all about his mastery of the material, you are only matching him up against other students. Most would recognize at core that the main purpose of grades is to compare one student against another. Most people are also aware that competition puts a strain on friendships and too often consigns students to a solitary journey.

Michelangelo is often quoted as having said that inside every block of stone or marble dwells a beautiful statue; one need only remove the excess material to reveal the work of art within. If we were to apply this visionary concept to education, it would be pointless to compare one child to another. Instead, all the energy would be focused on chipping away at the stone, getting rid of whatever is in the way of each child's developing skills, mastery, and self-expression.

We call this practice *giving an* A. It is an enlivening way of approaching people that promises to transform you as well as them. It is a shift in attitude that makes it possible for you to speak freely about your own thoughts and feelings while, at the same time, you support others to be all they dream of being. The practice of *giving an* A transports your relationships from the world of measurement into the universe of possibility.

An A can be given to anyone in any walk of life—to a waitress, to your employer, to your mother-in-law, to the members of the opposite team, and to the other drivers in traffic. When you give an A, you find yourself speaking to people not from a place of measuring how they stack up against your standards, but from a place of respect that gives them room to realize themselves. Your eye is on the statue within the roughness of the uncut stone.

This A is not an expectation to live up to, but a possibility to live into.

BRIGHT FUTURES

BEN: Thirty graduate students are gathered at the New England Conservatory for the first class of the year on a Friday afternoon in September. The students, all instrumentalists and singers, are about to undertake a two-semester exploration into the art of musical performance, including the psychological and emotional factors that can stand in the way of great music-making. I promise them that if they attend my Interpretation class regularly and apply themselves to mastering the distinctions that are put forward in the course, they will make major breakthroughs both in their music-making and in their lives.

Yet, after twenty-five years of teaching, I still came up against the same obstacle. Class after class, the students would be in such a chronic state of anxiety over the measurement of their perform-ance that they would be reluctant to take risks with their playing. One evening I settled down with Roz to see if we could think of something that would dispel their anticipation of failure.

What would happen if one were to hand an A to every student from the start?

Roz and I predicted that abolishing grades altogether would only make matters worse, even if the Conservatory could be per-suaded to support such a plan. The students would feel cheated of the opportunity for stardom and would still be focused on their place in the lineup. So we came up with the idea of giving them all the only grade that would put them at ease, not as a measure-ment tool, but as an instrument to open them up to possibility.

"Each student in this class will get an A for the course," I announce. "However, there is one requirement that you must ful-fill to earn this grade: Sometime during the next two weeks, you must write me a letter dated next May, which begins with the words, 'Dear Mr. Zander, I got my A because . . . ,' and in this let-ter you are to tell, in as much detail as you can, the story of what will have happened to you by next May that is in line with this extraordinary grade."

In writing their letters, I say to them, they are to place them-selves in the future, looking back, and to report on all the insights they acquired and milestones they attained during the year as if those accomplishments were already in the past. Everything must be written in the past tense. Phrases such as "I hope," "I intend," or "I will" must not appear. The students may, if they wish, mention specific goals reached or competitions won. "But, " I tell them, "I am especially interested in the *person* you will have become by next May. I am interested in the attitude, feelings, and worldview of that person who will have done all she wished to do or become everything he wanted to be." I tell them I want them to fall passionately in love with the person they are describing in their letter.

Here is one letter from a young trombonist who took that instruction to heart and discovered the poetry of self-invention.

Thursday 15 May, nighttime

Dear Mr. Z

Today the world knows me. That drive of energy and intense emotion that you saw twisting and dormant inside me, yet, alas, I could not show in performance or conversation, was freed tonight in a program of new music composed for me. . . . The concert ended and no one stirred. A pregnant quiet. Sighs: and then applause that drowned my heart's throbbing.

I might have bowed—I cannot remember now. The clapping sustained such that I thought I might make my debut complete and celebrate the shedding of

> *the mask and skin*
> *that I had constructed*
> *to hide within,*
> *by improvising on my own melody as an*
> *encore—unaccompanied. What followed is*
> *something of a blur. I forgot technique,*
> *pretension, tradition, schooling, history—*
> *truly even the audience.*
> *What came from my trombone*
> *I wholly believe, was my own*
> *Voice.*
> *Laughter, smiles,*
> *a frown, weeping*
> *Tuckerspirit*
> *did sing.*

Tucker Dulin

And here is another one of the A letters written by a young Korean flute player who entered wholeheartedly into the game, capturing perfectly its playfulness, while addressing in the process some of the most serious issues facing performers in a culture of measurement and competition.

Next May

Dearest Teacher Mr. Zander;

I received my grade A because I worked hard and thought hard about myself taking your class, and the result was absolutely tremendous. I became a new person. I used to be so negative person for almost everything even before trying. Now I find myself happier person than before. I couldn't accept my mistakes about a year ago, and after every mistake I blamed myself, but now, I enjoy making mistakes and I really learn from these mistakes. In my playing I have more depth than before. I used to play just notes, but, now, I found out about the real meaning of every pieces, and I could play with more imagination. Also I found out my value. I found myself so special person, because I found out that if I believe myself I can do everything. Thank you for all the lessons and lectures because that made me realize how important person I am and also the clear reason why I play music. Thank you,

Sincerely,
Esther Lee

In this letter, the young performer focuses her gaze on the person she wants to be, momentarily silencing the voice in her head that tells her that she will fail. She emerges like the graceful statue from within Michelangelo's marble block. The person that I teach each Friday afternoon is the person described in the letter. The student reveals her true self and also identifies much of the stone that blocks her expression. Chipping away at the stone that encases her becomes our task in the class. Our job is to remove the extraneous debris that stands between her and her expression in the world.

Next May

Dear Mr. Zander,

I got my A because I had the courage to examine my fears and I realized that they have no place in my life. I changed from someone who was scared to make a mistake in case she was noticed to someone who knows that she has a contribution to make to other people, musically and personally. . . . Thus all diffidence and lack of belief in myself are gone. So too is the belief that I only exist as a reflection in other people's eyes and the resulting desire to please everyone. . . . I understand that trying and achieving are the same thing when you are your own master—and I am.

I have found a desire to convey music to other people, which is stronger than the worries I had about myself. I have changed from desiring inconsequentiality and anonymity to accepting the joy that comes from knowing that my music changes the world.

—*Giselle Hillyer*

Small wonder that I approach each class with the greatest eagerness, for this is a class consisting entirely of A students and what is more delightful than spending an afternoon among the stars? Most members of the class share this experience, and some even report that as they walk down the corridor toward the classroom each Friday afternoon, the clouds of anxiety and despair that frequently shadow a hothouse American music academy perceptibly lift.

When I come to your class, Ben, I feel the glow coming as I walk down the corridor, and by the time I've arrived—I've arrived happy and excited and ready to go.

—*Carina*

We in the music profession train young musicians with utmost care from early childhood, urging them to achieve extraordinary technical mastery and encouraging them to develop good practice habits and performance values. We support them to attend fine summer programs and travel abroad to gain firsthand experience of different cultures, and then, after all this, we throw them into a maelstrom of competition, survival, backbiting, subservience, and status seeking. And from this arena we expect them to perform the great works of the musical literature that call upon, among other things, warmth, nobility, playfulness, generosity, reverence, sensitivity, and love!

It is dangerous to have our musicians so obsessed with competition because they will find it difficult to take the necessary risks with themselves to be great performers. The art of music, since it can only be conveyed through its interpreters, depends on expressive performance for its lifeblood. Yet it is only when we make mistakes in performance that we can really begin to notice what needs attention. In fact, I actively train my students that when they make a mistake, they are to lift their arms in the air, smile, and say, "How fascinating!" I recommend that everyone try this.

Not only mistakes, but even those experiences we ordinarily define as "negative" can be treated in this way. For instance, I once had a distraught young tenor ask to speak to me after class. He told me he'd lost his girlfriend and was in such despair that he was almost unable to function. I consoled him, but the teacher in me was secretly delighted. Now he would be able to fully express the heartrending passion of the song in Schubert's *Die Winterreise* about the loss of the beloved. That song had completely eluded him the previous week because up to then, the only object of affection he had ever lost was a pet goldfish.

My teacher, the great cellist Gaspar Cassadó, used to say to us as students, "I'm so sorry for you; your lives have been so easy. You can't play great music unless your heart's been broken."

Dear Mr. Zander,

I got my "A" because I became a great gardener to build my own garden of life. Till last year I was intimidated, judgmental, negative, lonely, lost, no energy to do what-so-ever, loveless, spiritless, hopeless, emotionless . . . endless. What I thought so miserably was actually what really made me to become what I am today, who loves myself, therefore music, life, people, my work, and even miseries. I love my weeds as much as my unblossomed roses. I can't wait for tomorrow because I'm in love with today, hard work, and reward . . . what can be better?

Sincerely,
Soyan Kim

THE SECRET OF LIFE

A few weeks into the first year of the *giving the* A experiment, I asked the class how it had felt to them to start the semester off with an A, before they had had to prove themselves in any way. To my surprise, a Taiwanese student put up his hand. Apart from a natural diffidence to speak up in a foreign language, it is rare for students from Asia, often among our most accomplished performers, to volunteer to speak in class. A few of the Asian students have tried to explain to me why this is so. In some Asian cultures, a high premium is traditionally put on being right. The teacher is always right, and the best way for students to avoid being wrong is not to say anything at all. So when this young student raised up his hand quite enthusiastically, of course I called on him.

"In Taiwan," he explained,

I was Number 68 out of 70 student. I come to Boston and Mr. Zander says I am an A. Very confusing. I walk about, three weeks, very confused. I am Number 68, but Mr. Zander says I am an A student . . . I am Number 68, but Mr. Zander says I

am an A. One day I discover much happier A than Number 68.
So I decide I am an A.

This student, in a brilliant flash, had hit upon the "secret of
life." He had realized that the labels he had been taking so seriously
are human inventions—it's all a game. The Number 68 is invented
and the A is invented, so we might as well choose to invent something that brightens our life and the lives of the people around us.

OFTEN PEOPLE ARE quite uncomfortable with the idea of
granting the unearned A because it seems to deny the actual differences between one person's accomplishments and another's.
We are not suggesting that people be blind to accomplishment.
Nobody wants to hear a violinist who cannot play the notes or to be
treated by a doctor who has not passed the course. Standards can
help us by defining the range of knowledge a student must master
to be competent in his field.

It is not in the context of measuring people's performance
against standards that we propose giving the A, despite the reference to measurement the A implies. We give the A to finesse the
stranglehold of judgment that grades have over our consciousness
from our earliest days. The A is an invention that creates possibility for both mentor and student, manager and employee, or for any
human interaction.

The practice of *giving the* A allows the teacher to line up with
her students in their efforts to produce the outcome, rather than
lining up with the standards against these students. In the first
instance, the instructor and the student, or the manager and the
employee, become a team for accomplishing the extraordinary; in
the second, the disparity in power between them can become a dis-
traction and an inhibitor, drawing energy away from productivity
and development.

One of the complications of working with standards is that
those in charge—be they teachers, school systems, CEOs, or

management teams—often fall into the trap of identifying their own agendas with the standards. How often in a business situation does a manager find himself at his wit's end when he discovers that work has not been done by others the way he would have done it himself? A common response is to deliver the ultimatum, whether explicitly or implicitly, "Do it the right way—my way."

Not only does this latter message tend to squelch innovation and creativity, but it also trains students and employees to focus solely on what they need to do to please their teachers or their bosses, and on how much they can get away with. The mentor's disappointment with a student whose style and interests vary from her own is often what is measured in the grade she gives. Instead of providing real information to a student on his learning, it tells him by how much, in the eyes of the authority, he has fallen short.

THE SENIOR PAPER

ROZ: As a high school student I clashed with my English Literature teacher in just this way over our senior project, a semester-long comprehensive study of one author's work. I was notorious for leaving papers and assignments until the very last minute, and this one was no exception. I had decided to write about Nathaniel Hawthorne; then, after reading most of his work, I changed my mind. It was only two or three weeks before the paper was due that I decided firmly on Thomas Hardy. I worked through the whole of the final night under what was for me a happy mixture of intense pressure and focused interest, and at school the next day I spent every free moment typing feverishly in the senior room. Predictably, at ten minutes to five, I submitted the completed draft to our teacher, receiving, like water off a duck's back, the requisite lecture on the folly of my organizational methods. The papers were to be graded by an outside reader, a teacher from another school who was unfamiliar with the students in our class.

For two weeks, the class awaited the results of our efforts with trepidation. Finally, the papers came back. Our teacher handed them out one by one, smiling at each student encouragingly. But when she came to me her expression was strained and unhappy. My anxiety shot up. In dread, I turned the paper over to see the comments on the back, but there, in soft dark pencil at the top of the page was a bold A. The reader praised the composition's ideas, organization, writing style, and grammar.

Our classroom teacher had a different agenda, presumably that students must learn to do their work at a certain pace, with certain preparatory documents. She said to me later, "I was very disappointed that you got such a high grade. I was hoping you would do badly so that you would learn a lesson about preparation." I felt as though I were being exiled from the sunny schoolyard where I had long played so enthusiastically. I began to defend my last-minute work style and to attach pride to habits that up to that point I had felt were simply a matter of personal style.

In retrospect, I am sure that my English teacher had my best interests at heart. She was probably worried that when things became tougher I would lack the skills to succeed. And she must have predicted that the A would validate my style, keeping me from ever trying a different approach. Yet, imagine if she had reacted to my A by giving me a "high five," and had invited me into a game: to try my hand at an outline well in advance of the due date of the next assignment, just to see if it would help me do an even better job. I know I would have agreed to play. By stepping down and meeting me in such an engaging and imaginative way, my teacher would have recovered the leadership role in my education. In our vocabulary, she would have given me an A, and, in the process, gained one for herself.

IN THE REALM of possibility, the literal or figurative giving of the A aligns teacher with student, manager with employee, and makes striving for a goal an enlivening game. Within the game, a standard becomes a marker that gives the pair direction. If the student hits the mark, the team is on course; if not, well, "How fascinating!" The instructor does not personally identify with the standard; nor does the student identify personally with the results of the game. Since the teacher's job is to help her students chip away at the barriers that block their abilities and expression, she aligns herself with the students to whom she has given an A, and lets the standards maintain themselves.

THE A BRINGS PEOPLE TOGETHER UNDER A COMMON PURPOSE

Even in a symphony orchestra, where the conductor and the hundred players have something collective at stake—namely a great performance—standards can wreak havoc. Not every conductor is capable of moving beyond his own agenda and his own prejudices to see how he supports or undermines the players' performance. Just before the oboist puts her reed to her lips for her big solo, she looks up at the conductor, and along with information about tempo, phrasing, shape, rhythm, color, and the character of the music, comes a message that includes a grade—and that, as much as anything else, will determine how she plays.

The freely granted A expresses a vision of partnership, teamwork, and relationship. It is for wholeness and functionality, in the awareness that for each of us, excess stone may still hide the graceful form within.

In the absence of a vision, we are each driven by our own agenda, finding people whose interests match ours, and inattentive to those with whom we appear to have little in common. We automatically judge our players, workers, and loved ones against our standards, inadvertently pulling the wind from their sails. But with our new practice of granting an ongoing A in all our relationships, we can align ourselves with others, because that A declares and sustains a life-enhancing partnership.

TANYA'S BOW

BEN: Throughout the rehearsal process of Mahler's Ninth Symphony with the Philharmonia Orchestra of London, I had been aware that one of the violinists had been sitting in an overly relaxed, almost slouched position. By the time of the dress rehearsal, her posture, still unchanged, was in noticeable contrast to the other players, who were now fired up and physically demonstrative. Although her playing was completely professional, the gut-wrenching intensity of Mahler's final testament made her indifferent manner, dispiriting in any performance, seem particularly incongruous in this one.

At the end of the rehearsal, I went up to her and asked whether anything was amiss. Her response surprised me. "Are these your bowings?" she inquired. When I told her that these were the bowings we had used in our last performance in Boston, she commented, "The music goes too fast for all these bow changes. I just cannot get into the string." Since I know how difficult it is to apply a fast-moving bow to the string with enough pressure to make a big sound, I suggested that perhaps we should take a slower tempo. But she was taken aback. "Don't be ridiculous," she remonstrated, "you should perform it the way you feel it. But you did ask."

This was a revelation to me. A player's outward demeanor, her whole physical appearance, even her mood, were connected to her comfort with the bowings! One should remember that the conductor of the orchestra is not actually playing the music, however attuned he or she is to each instrument—and as a string player, I consider myself particularly sensitive to the physical motions of the bow. However, in my eternal quest to find the right tempo for the music, in my desire to reveal the aching, arching long lines and the turbulent frenzy of Mahler's expression, I had probably been led to move the tempo somewhat faster, thereby sacrificing the player's vital kinesthetic relationship of bow to string. The cost was the discomfort and finally the resignation of a valued member of the violin section of one of the world's greatest orchestras. That was too high a price.

My usual routine on the day of a concert is to go to my room after the morning's rehearsal and take a long sleep, then shower, eat two English muffins and a scrambled egg with some nice strong English tea, and return to the hall to give my customary preconcert talk. This time, however, it all changed. I went back to my hotel room and spent the afternoon with Mahler's score, imagining how it would feel to play each passage on the violin. It was obviously not *all* too fast. Maybe this passage? Maybe that one? At the concert that evening, I slightly broadened each of the passages that I had decided might have presented a problem for Tanya's bow.

During the performance, I frequently glanced in her direction, and there in her seat was an impassioned, unabashedly demonstrative player totally enraptured by the music. Although we would have played a more than respectable performance without the full participation of Tanya, the engagement of that extra 1 percent caused a disproportionate breakthrough because once she and I were in relationship, I too could be fully present. When I had been viewing her as an unimportant casualty, I had to pretend it did not matter that for some reason she was not engaged. Meanwhile, I wasted energy both watching and ignoring her.

After the concert Tanya was nowhere to be found, but a few weeks later I decided to track her down to thank her for the last-minute coaching that had helped us give such a stirring and satisfying performance. I obtained her phone number from the Philharmonia office and called one morning from Boston to the London suburb where she lived.

Tanya seemed audibly shaken when I identified myself. She confessed that she had never received a call from a conductor at home before. She responded with delight as I expressed my deep gratitude for her contribution to our performance of Mahler's Ninth. It emerged that Mahler was her favorite composer, that she was passionate about all his work, and that the performance we had done together was one of the high points of her musical life.

The lesson I learned is that *the player who looks least engaged may be the most committed member of the group*. A cynic, after all, is a passionate person who does not want to be disappointed again. Tanya, the Mahlerian par excellence, had decided to "sit out" that performance because it was going to disappoint her again. I learned from Tanya that the secret is not to speak to a person's cynicism, but to speak to her passion.

When I initially approached Tanya—not to reprimand a recalcitrant member of the team for not pulling her weight, but rather with the attitude, the certain knowledge, that she loved the music, that she wanted the concert to be a success, that she wanted to "get into the string" with her bow—I gave her an A. My question to her, "Is there anything amiss?" was a question to someone I imagined to be completely committed to the project we were engaged in together, someone who, for whatever reason, was having a hard time.

When I returned to the Philharmonia the next season, Tanya greeted me enthusiastically. As a result of my experience with this violinist, it seemed that I had a warmer relationship with all the players there. During the break at one of the rehearsals of Mahler's Second, after we had been working on the subtly lilting, Viennese-waltz–like second movement, I slipped into the chair beside my new friend. "A tiny bit slow, don't you think?" she murmured.

THE PRACTICE OF *giving the* A both invents and recognizes a universal desire in people to contribute to others, no matter how many barriers there are to its expression. We can choose to validate the apathy of a boss, a player, or a high school student and become resigned ourselves, or we can choose to honor in them an unfulfilled yearning to make a difference. How often, for instance, do we see teenagers slumped into that same resigned position in which Tanya sat through those rehearsals? How differently would we understand and speak with them were we to hand them permanent, unqualified A's, without denying anything that happens in our dealings with them? Starting from the conviction that adolescents are looking for an arena in which to make an authentic contribution to the family and to the community, the first thing we would notice is how few meaningful roles are available for young people to fill. Then we might see how, in the absence of a purpose greater than themselves, adolescents retreat to the sidelines as though their existence were inconsequential.

SECOND FIDDLE-ITIS: THE HABIT OF THINKING YOU MAKE NO DIFFERENCE

BEN: After the initial discussion and excitement over the A subsides, I predict to the students in my Friday class that it will not be long before a voice in their heads will whisper something along these lines:

> *Why should I bother to go to class today? I already have my A. And I've got so much to do; I really need to practice on my own. Anyway, it's such a large class, he probably won't even notice.*

I tell the students that this is the first symptom of a widespread disease called "second fiddle-itis," popularly known as "playing second fiddle." People who perceive their role in a group to be of little significance (second violins for example) are particularly vulnerable to its ravages. The string players in an orchestra often see themselves as redundant foot soldiers, virtual cannon fodder for the egotistical whim of the conductor. Many other players, after all, duplicate their part. This is not true for the lead trumpet or the main wind players, who are soloists within the orchestra.

A string player just entering a new position in an orchestra will often start off with great enthusiasm, take his part home at night, and continue to do careful and regular practice in his spare time. However, when it begins to dawn on him that his stand partner stopped practicing years ago and that the conductor does not seem to care or even to hear when players are out of tune, he too quickly begins to show signs of the onset of the disease.

A first oboist, on the other hand, is unlikely to give up making reeds or to miss a rehearsal. It is simply too noticeable. In all my years of conducting, I do not believe I have ever known a first oboe to be late for a rehearsal. Is it because the oboe has to be there at the beginning to tune everyone to the A?

"So," I tell the class, "the next time you hear the little second-violin melody in your head that says, *'I'm not going to class because I'm too tired,'* or *'I have too much to do, and I know it won't make any difference anyway'*—remember that you are an A student. An A student is a leading player in any class, an integral voice, and the class cannot make its music without that voice."

Once, in Spain, I saw a big sign outside a little shop. It read:

ALVAREZ
Shoemaker
and
Lessons in
Second Violin

I found myself hoping that Alvarez's great humility did not irrevocably limit the aspirations of his students.

However, when I myself had the privilege of playing string quartets with Robert Koff, the founding second violinist of the Julliard String Quartet, I came away convinced that the real leader of the string quartet *is* the second violin. Not because Koff dominated the rest of us, but because in his part he had all the inner rhythms and harmonies, and he gave them such clarity and authority that we were all tremendously influenced by his playing. He was leading us from the "seconds." In a truly great string quartet, all four players are doing that simultaneously.

ROZ: One year, part way into the second semester, Ben asked me to teach his graduate class at the Conservatory while he was conducting in Europe. The students were always interested in learning new techniques for dealing with stage nerves, and he felt I had something important to offer them on that subject.

However, as I was driving to the Conservatory, I was dismayed to find that *I* was the one who was unaccountably nervous. My thoughts flew with horror to the next two hours: I pictured myself in front of the class, white-faced and shaken, while we discussed the students' performance anxiety. This was likely to be completely humiliating.

The first thing I did was attempt to manage the fear: I instructed myself to "stay with the emotion," an idea that proved singularly unhelpful. Then I berated myself for not being able to handle my own anxiety.

It did not occur to me to look to see what grade I was giving the graduate students I was about to address.

When I stepped in front of the class, I was still intensely anxious and self-absorbed, but as I started to speak, things shifted. "I'm thrilled to be here," I said (a lie in transition toward the truth), "because . . . (I didn't yet know what I was going to say) . . . because you are a group of artists . . . and I couldn't possibly have a better audience for a discussion of a subject in which I have a passionate interest: creativity."

And suddenly it was all true. Once I had given my audience an A and invented them as colleagues, they were *precisely* the people with whom I wanted to converse, and I was *exactly* where I wanted to be. If we really do have the choice of saying who is in the class we are teaching, or the orchestra we are conducting, or the group we are managing, why would we ever define them as people we cannot effectively and enjoyably work with?

Time flew as this A class invented stories to live and work by, stories that enhanced their passion and creativity. The answer to the mystery of stage nerves turned out to be the same as the secret of life: it's all a matter of invention.

GIVING AN A is a fundamental, paradigmatic shift toward the realization that it is all invented—the A is invented and the Number 68 is invented, and so are all the judgments in between. Some readers might conclude that our practice is merely an exercise in "putting a positive spin" on a negative opinion, or "thinking the best of someone," and "letting bygones be bygones." But that is not it at all. No behavior of the person to whom you assign an A need be whitewashed by that grade, and no action is so bad that behind it you cannot recognize a human being to whom you can speak the truth. You can grant the proverbial ax murderer an A by addressing him as a person who knows he has forfeited his humanity and lost all control, and you can give your sullen, lazy, secretive teenager an A, and she will still at that moment be sleeping the morning away. When she awakes, however, the conversation between you and her will go a little differently because she will have become for you a person whose true nature is to participate—however blocked she may be. And you will know you are communicating with her, even if you see that she is tongue-tied or too confused to answer you just then.

When we give an A we can be open to a perspective different from our own. For after all, it is only to a person to whom you have granted an A that you will really listen, and it is in that rare instance when you have ears for another person that you can truly appreciate a fresh point of view.

In the measured context of our everyday lives, the grades we hand out often rise and fall with our moods and opinions. We may disagree with someone on one issue, lower their grade, and never quite hear what they have to say again. Each time the grade is altered, the new assessment, like a box, defines the limits of what is possible between us.

MAHLER AND KATRINE

BEN: A member of my orchestra demonstrated the miracles that can happen when you drop all your limiting assumptions about a child's interests and understanding, without applying expectations of any kind.

The Boston Philharmonic had scheduled a fall performance of Mahler's Ninth Symphony, and because of the extraordinary difficulty of the music I decided to send a tape of the piece out to every member of the orchestra, so they could get to know it over the summer. One of our violinists, Anne Hooper, took the tape with her to an island off the coast of Maine, where she was visiting with her family, and played it on her boom box.

Her five-year-old niece, Katrine, stopped to listen for a while, and then asked, "Auntie Anne, what is this music about?" Anne set out to weave a wondrous tale for the little girl, telling her a story about a wild and fearsome dragon and a beautiful princess who is locked up in a castle. For the duration of the ninety-minute symphony, Anne spun her tale of the princess and her handsome prince.

The following day, little Katrine asked to hear the music about the beautiful princess again. So once again Anne put on the tape and let it run its course, only occasionally reminding Katrine of her invented story line.

When the piece was playing for the third time at Katrine's request, about halfway through she asked, "Auntie Anne, what is this music *really* about?"

Anne regarded her five-year-old niece with astonishment, and then began to tell her the true story of Mahler—how sad his life was, how he'd lost seven brothers and sisters from sickness during his childhood so that the coffin became a regular piece of furniture in his house. She told Katrine how cruel his alcoholic father had been to him, and how frightened his invalid mother. She told her that Mahler's little daughter had died at the age of four, that he never really got over that loss, and that he'd been forced to quit his important job at the famous Opera House in Vienna because he was Jewish. "And then, just before he wrote this symphony," Anne said, "Mahler was told by his doctor that he had a weak heart and only a very short time to live. So now, Mahler was really saying good-bye to everything and looking back over his life. That is why so much of the music is so sad and why at the end of the piece it dies out to nothing—it's a description of his death as he imagined it, his final breath."

Anne went on to explain that Mahler wasn't sad all the time. He was a great lover of nature and a powerful swimmer and he loved to walk. He had a magnificent laugh and a huge love of life, and all this is in the music too, as well as his sadness and anger about his illness and the brutality of his father and the vulnerability of his invalid mother. In fact, Mahler thought that he should put everything in life in his symphonies—so anything that can be imagined can be heard in them if you listen carefully enough.

The next day, Katrine came running up to her aunt and said, "Auntie Anne, Auntie Anne, can we listen to that music about the man again today?" Well they did, and again the next day, and in fact Katrine's parents told me that she listened to it nearly one hundred times that summer. The following October, the entire family made the four-hour drive from upstate New York to Boston to hear our performance in Jordan Hall. Katrine sat wide-eyed through the whole piece. Later, she wrote me a thank-you note.

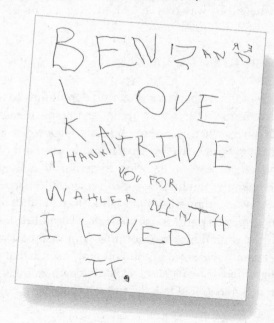

I carry this note with me everywhere I go. It reminds me how seldom we pay attention to, or even look for, the passionate and the extraordinary in children—how seldom we give children an A.

WHEN HE RETIRED from the Supreme Court, Justice Thurgood Marshall was asked of what accomplishment he was most proud. He answered, simply, "That I did the best I could with what I had." Could there be any greater acknowledgment? He gave himself an A, and within this framework he was free to speak of errors of judgment, of things he would have done differently had he had access to other views.

Giving yourself an A is not about boasting or raising your self-esteem. It has nothing to do with reciting your accomplishments. The freely granted A lifts you off the success/failure ladder and spirits you away from the world of measurement into the universe of possibility. It is a framework that allows you to see all of who you are and *be* all of who you are, without having to resist or deny any part of yourself.

RECONSTRUCTING OUR PAST

The pathway of the A offers us a profound opportunity to transform our personal histories. It allows us to reevaluate the grades we assigned to others when we were children, grades that affect our lives now, as legends we live by. How often do we stand convinced of the truth of our early memories, forgetting that they are but assessments made by a child? We can replace the narratives that hold us back by inventing wiser stories, free from childish fears, and, in doing so, disperse long-held psychological stumbling blocks.

Usually the impetus for transforming your own past will come from a feeling of hopelessness in the present, a sense that you have been through the same frustrating experience time and again. Our analytic powers don't seem to help, though some of us never weary of exercising them. The people we are involved with seem so fixed in their ways. How can we get them to change? We tend not to notice our own hand in this ill-starred situation, so rarely are we looking in a productive place for the answer. Why not give some attention to the grades we are handing out?

ROZ AND HER FATHER

ROZ: I discovered this some years ago, after a wearyingly familiar argument with my husband, one that left us both irritable and a little desperate. I used the moment, alone with myself, to go down the path of the A, rather than to follow the usual route of reproach and blame. Well-trained to look into the past for the source of current interpretations, I asked myself what grade I'd given the first man in my life, my father, and why. My father had been dead a dozen years, but with his memory came the marks I'd given him.

My parents had separated shortly after my birth, and my contact with my father had been sporadic from then on. He lived with his new wife and child nearby, until I was six or seven years old. My older sister and I would visit him every other week or so, but when he took his new family across the country, our contact dwindled. I waited two years after my sister had gone with him to Florida on a deep-sea fishing adventure to ask him to take *me* on a solo journey. I was eight. He turned me down. In my teens I tried again, with an unsatisfying outcome: my request resulted in a generic invitation to my sister as well. Not until I was eighteen did I finally get a chance to spend time with my father on my own.

When I was in my twenties, I would visit with him briefly whenever he passed though New York City, en route to some other destination. Things were not working out for him the way he had hoped. He had looked forward to retirement and a life of leisure in Florida, but when it came, it seemed not to have fulfilled its promise. We got the shocking news that he had died suddenly, by his own hand, at the age of sixty-five.

Sitting in an armchair years later, I asked myself some basic questions. Do I think he had loved me? No. But, to be fair, how could he have? He hardly knew me. That was the problem, I had always thought, so little one-on-one contact. And what grade had I given him? B–, maybe C. On what basis? Because he hadn't made the effort to get to know me, his own daughter. He hadn't known me and he hadn't loved me. Had he known me, had he taken the time to get to know me, he would have loved me.

Sitting there reflecting on this, I recognized what an appalling premise I had been operating under—though ostensibly so real—that my father had not loved me. I looked to see whether I had brought this assumption to other relationships and found that indeed I had. In fact, I recognized that it was the box that every intimate relationship of mine had come packaged in. And when I felt unloved, had I striven patiently to make known my desires and to be understood and acknowledged? Absolutely, in every case. And always I had been left with a feeling of failure.

Could the practice of *giving an* A do anything for my father and me? Could it get us out of this box? I would probably have to start with the notion that he had loved me, at least somewhat, but where would I go from there? How would I explain the facts?

Here is how I gave him an A. I said:

He loved me.

"Well," I told myself, "if I'm willing to say that he loved me, I can grant that he knew me, at least somewhat."

He loved me;
He knew me.

Why then had he not wanted to be with me?
Why had we lost contact?

An answer unfolded from the new premises:

He loved me;
He knew me;
He felt he had nothing to offer me.

Of course. My father was not happy with himself. Who would take himself so thoroughly away from the world, but a person who felt he had nothing of value to offer?

For the first time, tears sprung to my eyes for him—or for us, I couldn't tell which—but they were not tears of self-pity. The rearrangement of meaning seemed to me more real, and attuned to a wiser part of me, than the story I had previously sworn by. I looked at other relationships I had had and saw how absurd it was to characterize a man who had chosen a partnership with me as not loving me and not knowing me. And furthermore, how exhausting to feel I had to work so hard for recognition and acknowledgment!

I began to write a different narrative: that my husband did indeed know me and love me, and was offering me the best he had to give. Then when I talked with him, I spoke from within the framework of the A, to someone I had defined as able and willing to hear me. As long as I practiced in this manner, I found that virtually all the conversations we had were productive in a way I had never before imagined they could be.

A few days after rethinking my relationship with my father, I was rummaging through a box of books I had found in the basement, when a letter slipped out and fell resolutely to my feet. It was in my father's hand, dated some twenty years previously. I looked at it as though I had never seen it before; indeed, I would have said that I had never received a letter from my father in my entire life.

Dear Rosamund,

It was wonderful to see you. I hope you choose a profession that involves working with and helping others, because I think you are really talented at that.

Love, Father

He knew me exactly the way I would have wanted to be known.

It works that way. As soon as you have the grace to give people A's, all sorts of things are revealed that were as though hidden behind a veil. Letters pop out, memories return. There are new openings. When the relationship itself is no longer in question, we can ask ourselves, what now do we want to create?

MANY OF US suffer from the conviction that our parents withheld from us an A. Often the advice we receive, delivered with an earnest, pitying look is, "You can't change people," though most of us will go to our graves trying. That adage is true, of course, in the world of measurement, where people and things are fixed in character. However, in the universe of possibility, you certainly *can* change people. They change as you speak. You may ask, "Who, actually, is doing the changing?" And the answer is *the relationship*. Because in the arena of possibility, everything occurs in that context.

Here is a letter from a man who heard about the practice of the A, gave way to the power of music, and transformed his life, all in the space of an afternoon.

My Dear Benjamin Zander,

You have just completed a presentation to the leadership of the North Shore–Long Island Jewish Health System. I "should" be immediately returning to my job as one of the System's Vice Presidents (such a fancy title, no?), but not without first sitting down and briefly telling you of how your words, energy, and humour affected me this day.

I am the man who approached you and told you of my emotional "reunion" with my father through your presentation. He was Swiss-German, and throughout my adult life I have struggled to explain to myself why, in the 25 years that he was with me, he could never, even once, say to me "I love you." Oh, we did many things as a family, and I suppose his "teachings" in the form of admonishments have always remained with me, though softened, as I had the joy of becoming a father myself to 5 beautiful children.

You told us, as you were about to play Chopin, to use the time to reflect on someone no longer in our lives. I thought about my father and again about that nagging question which I could never answer—why couldn't he say "I love you"?

And then, as if delivered by a bolt of lightning, I recalled an incident that occurred between us at least 45 years ago. I was an asthmatic child, and on so many evenings could not run to the door (as instructed to do by our mother) to say hello to my father and give him a hug and a kiss when he came home late each evening from the hotel kitchens. I would instead remain upstairs, bedridden, gasping for every breath, waiting expectantly for Father to come upstairs and just say hello to me and maybe, just maybe, for the first time, say "Hello, Jeanot, I love you." But those words never came.

And then, as I listened to your music, the memory came back of an evening, more than 45 years ago, when I was again sick, and Father came upstairs. But this evening was different. He sat next to me on my bed and, as I was sitting upright and struggling for the next breath, he began gently stroking my hair for a period of time that I wished would have lasted an eternity.

Today, as you played us the Chopin, tears came to my eyes. It struck me that while Father could not say these words, "I love you," they were expressed even more poignantly in the gentle stroking of a little boy's hair by his father's powerful hands. I recall that as he sat with me my asthma attack subsided.

I had completely forgotten that incident. I must have buried it in my own desire to perhaps keep my father at a distance, to continuously prove either that I was unlovable, or that he was just a cold s.o.b. who only knew work, work, and more work. But not so. My father showed me love in so many ways.

We keep looking so hard in life for the "specific message," and yet we are blinded to the fact that the message is all around us, and within us all the time. We just have to stop demanding that it be on OUR terms or conditions, and instead open ourselves to the possibility that what we seek may be in front of us all the time.

Thank you,
John Imhof

THE ONLY GRACE *you can have is the grace you can imagine.*
An A radiates possibility through a family, a workplace, and a community, gaining strength, bringing joy and expression and a flowering of talent and productivity. Who knows how far it will travel?
An old parable adds a touch of grace to the practice of giving an A.

The Monks' Story

*A monastery has fallen on hard times. It was once part of a great
order which, as a result of religious persecution in the seven-
teenth and eighteenth centuries, lost all its branches. It was dec-
imated to the extent that there were only five monks left in the
mother house: the Abbot and four others, all of whom were over
seventy. Clearly it was a dying order.*

*Deep in the woods surrounding the monastery was a little
hut that the Rabbi from a nearby town occasionally used for a
hermitage. One day, it occurred to the Abbot to visit the hermitage to see if the Rabbi could offer any advice that might save
the monastery. The Rabbi welcomed the Abbot and commiser-
ated. "I know how it is," he said, "the spirit has gone out of people. Almost no one comes to the synagogue anymore." So the old
Rabbi and the old Abbot wept together, and they read parts of
the Torah and spoke quietly of deep things.*

*The time came when the Abbot had to leave. They
embraced. "It has been wonderful being with you," said the
Abbot, "but I have failed in my purpose for coming. Have you
no piece of advice that might save the monastery?" "No, I am
sorry," the Rabbi responded, "I have no advice to give. The only
thing I can tell you is that the Messiah is one of you."*

*When the other monks heard the Rabbi's words, they won-
dered what possible significance they might have. "The Messiah
is one of us? One of us, here, at the monastery? Do you suppose
he meant the Abbot? Of course—it must be the Abbot, who has
been our leader for so long. On the other hand, he might have
meant Brother Thomas, who is undoubtably a holy man. Certainly he couldn't have meant Brother Elrod—he's so crotchety.
But then Elrod is very wise. Surely, he could not have meant
Brother Phillip—he's too passive. But then, magically, he's*

always there when you need him. Of course he didn't mean me—yet supposing he did? Oh Lord, not me! I couldn't mean that much to you, could I?"

As they contemplated in this manner, the old monks began to treat each other with extraordinary respect, on the off chance that one of them might be the Messiah. And on the off off chance that each monk himself might be the Messiah, they began to treat themselves with extraordinary respect.

Because the forest in which it was situated was beautiful, people occasionally came to visit the monastery, to picnic or to wander along the old paths, most of which led to the dilapidated chapel. They sensed the aura of extraordinary respect that surrounded the five old monks, permeating the atmosphere. They began to come more frequently, bringing their friends, and their friends brought friends. Some of the younger men who came to visit began to engage in conversation with the monks. After a while, one asked if he might join. Then another, and another. Within a few years, the monastery became once again a thriving order, and—thanks to the Rabbi's gift—a vibrant, authentic community of light and love for the whole realm.

Being a

Contribution

Strolling along the edge of the sea, a man catches sight of a young woman who appears to be engaged in a ritual dance. She stoops down, then straightens to her full height, casting her arm out in an arc. Drawing closer, he sees that the beach around her is littered with starfish, and she is throwing them one by one into the sea. He lightly mocks her: "There are stranded starfish as far as the eye can see, for miles up the beach. What difference can saving a few of them possibly make?" Smiling, she bends down and once more tosses a starfish out over the water, saying serenely, "It certainly makes a difference to this one."

FROM OUR EARLIEST DAYS, we understand that there are tasks ahead of us to accomplish and landmarks to achieve. Life often looks like an obstacle course. In order to maximize success, we spend a good deal of time discussing what stands in the way of it. The man in the story sees only obstacles when he speaks of the countless starfish. He warns the young woman that her gestures are futile. Too many starfish, not enough time, not enough staff or resources, results too difficult to track . . .

The story as told, however, reveals nothing about the "success" or "failure" of the rescue mission, or what proportion of the starfish survived or perished. It does not describe the past, nor foretell the future. All we hear is that the young woman was smiling and serene, and that she moved in the pattern of a dance. Absent are the familiar measurements of progress. Instead, life is revealed as a place to contribute and we as contributors. Not because we have done a measurable amount of good, but because that is the story we tell.

THE DINNER TABLE GAME

BEN: I grew up in a traditional Jewish household, which meant, apart from much warmth and chicken soup, an assumption that all the children would be "successful." It was never openly articulated, but it was implied in many family interactions.

Each evening at the dinner table, for instance, with my parents seated at either end, and we four children between, my father would turn to my eldest brother and say, "What did you do today?" And my brother would describe, at what seemed to me considerable length, all the things he'd accomplished. Then my second brother would be asked the same question, and then my sister. By the time it came to me, I would be a nervous wreck, because usually I didn't think what I had done that day was very significant. Moreover, I realized that the question being asked was not really, "What did you do today?" but "What did you achieve today?" And I thought I hadn't achieved nearly as much as my very accomplished siblings. So I grew up with an undertow of anxiety that lasted into my middle age.

The drive to be successful and the fear of failure are, like the head and tail of a coin, inseparably linked. They goaded me on to unusual efforts and caused me, and those around me, considerable suffering. Of course, the surprising thing was that my increasing success did little to lessen the tension.

Until the splash of cold water. My second wife walked away from the marriage midstream.

At the same time she asserted—though at first I did not listen—that we would always be in relationship, and that it was up to us to invent the form. Clearly the family had not been thriving under the arrangement we'd had. "Let's invent a form," she said, "that allows us to contribute to each other, and let's set a distance that supports us to be fully ourselves." Going down for the second time, I understood and grabbed hold. I saw the whole thing was made up and that the game of success was just that, a game. I realized I could invent another game.

I settled on a game called *I am a contribution*. Unlike success and failure, *contribution* has no other side. It is not arrived at by comparison. All at once I found that the fearful question, "Is it enough?" and the even more fearful question, "Am I loved for who I am, or for what I have accomplished?" could both be replaced by the joyful question, "How will I be a *contribution* today?"

When I was a boy playing the dinner table game, and later an adult playing the success/failure game, I constantly judged myself by what I believed to be other people's standards. Nothing was ever quite good enough. There was always another orchestra—aside from the one I was conducting—that I suspected would bring me more success, and so I was never really present when I was on the podium. When I used to go out on dates, I would find myself looking over my shoulder for someone better. Too much of what I did was measured by the success that I might gain, so I rarely had peace, either professionally or in my private life.

As a conductor, I often drove the players and the administrators to realize my ambition, and no matter how much support I received, I still found myself distrustful. The game I was in was a competitive one, and in this game you can make alliances with people who are on your side, whose objectives are the same as yours; but you cannot rely on anyone who is aiming toward anything else, lest it detract from what you want for yourself.

When I began playing the game of *contribution*, on the other hand, I found there was no better orchestra than the one I was conducting, no better person to be with than the one I was with; in fact, there was no "better." In the game of *contribution* you wake up each day and bask in the notion that you are a gift to others.

In this new game, it is not as though the question of where you stand disappears, or how important you are, or how much money you hope to make. However, just for the moment, those concerns are packed away in a box of another name, where life operates under a different set of rules.

WHEN, IN THIS BOOK, we refer to various activities of life as "games," we do not mean to imply that these activities are frivolous or make no difference. We are simply pointing to the fact that any accepted model for doing things comes with an implicit set of rules, and that these rules govern our behavior just as surely as the rules of baseball govern the movements of the players on the field.

When people play a game, they agree to a certain set of limitations to create a challenge. In baseball, a batter tries to hit the ball, but it only *counts* as a hit if the ball lands within the 90-degree angle formed by the first and third baselines, is not caught in the air, is not fielded and thrown to first base before the batter gets there, is not used to tag the batter out or get a third out elsewhere on the field, and on and on. In *Scrabble*, a player seeks to attach a word at the spot on the board that will bring him the most points, but he can use only the seven letters in his hand and the words he spells must appear in the dictionary.

Half the fun of playing games like baseball—or the kind that come in a box—is that they challenge us to adapt and hone our skills to win in a distinctive environment that itself can be packed away, or left, once the game is over. Then we can shake hands, set up a rematch, or move on to the next event. It is the nature of games to provide alternative frameworks for engagement and expression and growth, whisking us away from the grimmer context in which we hold the everyday.

The purpose of describing, say, your professional life or your family traditions as a game is twofold. You instantly shift the context from one of survival to one of opportunity for growth. You also have the choice of imagining other games you might prefer to play in these realms. Naming your activities as a game breaks their hold on you and puts you in charge.

Just look carefully at the cover of the box, and if the rules do not light up your life, put it away, take out another one you like better, and play the new game wholeheartedly. Remember, *it's all invented.*

THE PRACTICE

The practice of this chapter is inventing oneself as a *contribution*, and others as well. The steps to the practice are these:

1. Declare yourself to be a *contribution*.

2. Throw yourself into life as someone who makes a difference, accepting that you may not understand how or why.

The *contribution* game appears to have remarkable powers for transforming conflicts into rewarding experiences.

TWO GENERATIONS OF GENEROSITY

ROZ: One couple I counseled played a very dreary game for years, until they discovered the game of *contribution*. Robert and Marianne were both in academic fields, and money, or rather the lack of it, was a nagging problem for them. They had one child already in college and one on her way, and even with the best planning, they always seemed to come up short when tax time rolled around.

Marianne's mother was quite well-to-do, but leaned toward a Calvinist philosophy of frugality and financial independence. Each April, Marianne would find herself, as she put it, "crawling home" to her mother to ask for enough money to make up the shortfall. And every year, her mother would lecture her on her failure in planning, before grudgingly giving Marianne what she had asked for.

I had been working with Marianne for about six months when her taxes came due. She arrived at our session dreading the annual visit to her mother, this time to ask for two thousand dollars. That was the very least she and her husband had calculated they would need in order to get by. She was angry with herself for being in this situation, and angry with her mother for making it so difficult to ask for help. She found it hard not to resent the fact that her mother lived in leisure with such wealth, while each of her daughters struggled to make ends meet. I thought about her predicament from the point of view of the *contribution* game.

"Do you suppose your mother *likes* to see you whining and groveling for money?" I asked Marianne. "Do you think it will be satisfying to her to hand out two thousand dollars, and still leave you miserable, and battling to pay your bills?"

Marianne shook her head and looked up, holding back tears.

"What is the sum of money that would make a real difference, that would give you and your family ease in your lives and in planning for the future?" I watched her face struggle to address the question. The sum that eventually lit up her countenance was twenty times the amount she had been prepared to request.

I asked Marianne to consider not only the *contribution* her mother would be making to the well-being of her family by giving her that amount of money, but more important, the *contribution* Marianne herself might be in her mother's life, as a daughter whose family was no longer at the brink of financial disaster. It wasn't easy for her to change her viewpoint, to think of herself as a contributory member of her extended family instead of a failure. But that was the challenge.

She took the risk. She went to see her mother that weekend, determined to show her enthusiasm over the life she envisioned for herself and her family, and alive to a possibility for all the generations in offering her mother the chance to help her realize it.

"How did it go?" I asked when I saw Marianne next, but I knew the answer from the way she carried herself. She'd had the best visit of her adult life. Her mother had leapt at the opportunity to do something demonstrably positive for her daughter.

"But that's only half the story," Marianne said, laughing. "When I got back home, there were messages on my answering machine from both of my sisters, wanting to know what had gotten into our mother—she had given each of them an equal sum of money out of the blue!"

WHEN YOU PLAY the *contribution* game, it is never a single individual who is transformed. Transformation overrides the divisions of identity and possession that are the architecture of the measurement model, recasting the tight pattern of scarcity into a widespread array of abundance.

LIKE RIPPLES IN A POND

BEN: After I experienced the joy of redefining my work as a place of *contribution* rather than an arena for my success, I began to think about a way of introducing my students at the Conservatory to the game. I decided to give them another assignment during the first class of the year, in addition to writing the A letter. I now ask them to take a moment in that class to write down how they have "contributed" over the past week. They naturally assume that I mean musically, how have they contributed musically, but I explain that they should jot down *anything* they said or did that they are willing to call a *contribution*—from helping an old lady cross the street to setting their boyfriends straight.

This exercise has a startling effect on how the students think of themselves. There is no place in it for them to talk about how little they practice, or to tell a story of how irresponsible or unkind they have been. They are only to describe themselves in the light of *contribution*. The assignment for the week after is to notice how they are a *contribution* as the week goes by—they are just to notice, not to do anything about it—and then come back and share what they saw with the class. The third assignment is to cast themselves as a *contribution* into the week ahead, like a pebble into a pond, and imagine that everything they do sends ripples out beyond the horizon.

There is an aspect of psychological practicing in these exercises parallel to the technical practicing my students do on their instruments. It is a discipline of the spirit. In order to be a great performer, you have to be unfettered by stage nerves. These exercises in *contribution* are a way of oiling the machinery to make one a more effective vehicle to convey the message of Brahms or Beethoven.

I tell my students, "Imagine you are pianist and you meet someone who has no familiarity with—perhaps has never even heard—the E-Minor Prelude of Chopin. You might want to sit down next to him at the piano and say, 'Listen to the theme in the right hand. See how it holds together over the arch of four bars, and then the melody goes down one step? Listen to the constantly changing harmonies in the left hand, how they ring every possible change on the melody note . . . and so on.' As you get caught up in the excitement of explaining and sharing the music with your companion, would you have time to be nervous? Of course not! It wouldn't occur to you. But this is exactly what you are doing when you perform—you are pointing to the beauty and artistry of the music."

Rachel Mercer, a student in my class at the New England Conservatory, wrote this letter at the end of the semester:

I am now able to use the possibility that my every act can affect the world to communicate with people in such a way so that a wave of inspiration and happiness can flow throughout the world. I know now that music is not about fingers or bows or strings, but rather a connective vibration flowing through all human beings, like a heartbeat. It is my job and ambition to keep that invisible and easily cut lifeline free and supported in all parts of life . . .

NAMING ONESELF and others as a *contribution* produces a shift away from self-concern and engages us in a relationship with others that is an arena for making a difference. Rewards in the *contribution* game are of a deep and enduring kind, though less predictable than the trio of money, fame, and power that accrue to the winner in the success game. You never know what they will be, or from whence they will come.

SARAH'S MOVE

BEN: A young woman who had heard me give a talk, rang me up to ask if I would come to speak to the residents at a nearby Jewish home for the elderly. I saw in my diary that I was free on the afternoon of the date she mentioned, but I was engaged with so many other projects, including a concert on the weekend, that I knew it was foolish to add one more thing. However, the memory of my father living out the end of his life in an institution like this one overrode my common sense, and I accepted the invitation.

The day arrived without my having given it further thought, and now the pressure was even greater than I had feared. I had just flown into Boston from Washington that morning, and with talks, lectures, classes, and a concert to prepare, the last thing in the world I thought I needed was to waste a precious afternoon with a bunch of old people. I made an attempt to cancel the engagement, but the young woman expressed such disappointment on behalf of the residents that, once again, remembering my father, I agreed to come . . . on the condition that I be allowed to leave at three o'clock sharp. The talk was to begin at two.

Only one person was sitting in the fifth row of a bank of folding chairs when I walked into the rather dingy hall at ten minutes to two. She identified herself as Sarah. I chatted with her a moment and then asked her to move up to a seat nearer the front. Sarah stood her ground. "I always sit here," she said. I challenged her good-naturedly, "Who knows, Sarah, if you change your seat maybe something new will happen today."

Sarah took up the gauntlet. "Are you crazy? At my age? I'm eighty-three!" By now she was standing, and, as if to prove me wrong, she moved, from the fifth row to the fourth. I briefly considered the odds that no one else would arrive, and that I had put aside so many pressing affairs to talk only to Sarah, but gradually, the remaining chairs filled. By shortly after two o'clock, a sizable group was ready to begin. Sarah, it turned out, was by no means the oldest; one member of the audience was 103. The topic was "New Possibilities."

I told numerous stories, many of them about my father, who maintained Old World grace and values to the end of his life, though completely blind. My father had endured devastating experiences in his life—as a foot soldier in World War I, and as a man who in 1938 made the agonizing decision to move his own family from Germany to England, leaving his reluctant mother and aunts behind. The women who refused to leave were killed in the camps. I once asked him why he wasn't angry. He said, "I discovered a person cannot live a full life under the shadow of bitterness." Indeed, he won the affection of the residents and staff of his own senior center, Croham Leigh, because of his ability to throw a new light on any situation. "There is no such thing as bad weather," he used to say, "only inappropriate clothing." Even on his final day, Dad managed to make a paradigm-shifting joke. He was lying on his bed, devoid of all capacities except his ability to hear and to speak and his sense of humor. My brother Luke, who was his doctor, entered the room and announced his presence. The dying patient said to his physician: "Is there anything I can do to help?" and faintly chuckled. Those may well have been his last words. He died that evening.

We talked of many things that afternoon in the home for the elderly in Boston. Our laughter and singing, fifty strong, ignited the air in the once-dingy room. We challenged assumptions about old age and pointed toward some new beginnings.

At half past three, I opened the floor to questions. There were many. One lady asked in a heavy German Jewish accent, "Vy do you bother to come here? You're a talented young man. Vy do you vaste your time vit a bunch of old people like us?"

Quite taken aback, I confessed that earlier in the day, I had asked myself exactly the same question. "But so much has happened since then . . . ," I began. I searched for words to explain the intense involvement, the excitement, and the peace I felt at that moment. My eyes lit on Sarah. "When I walked in here, Sarah was in the fifth row, and now she is in the fourth!" And Sarah stood, raised her fist, and cried, "You ain't seen nothing yet! I just got started!" Then all of us began to clap, and we clapped and clapped and clapped. The applause went far beyond the point of clapping for Sarah. We were clapping for the joy of being alive.

As I walked out of that room, the clock said ten minutes to four. I was walking on air, and I had time for everything. The whole experience was one of radiating possibility.

Later, I remembered a parable my father used to tell that speaks of our limited understanding of the nature of the gifts the universe holds in store for us.

Four young men sit by the bedside of their dying father. The old man, with his last breath, tells them there is a huge treasure buried in the family fields. The sons crowd around him crying, "Where, where?" but it is too late. The day after the funeral and for many days to come, the young men go out with their picks and shovels and turn the soil, digging deeply into the ground from one end of each field to the other. They find nothing and, bitterly disappointed, abandon the search.

The next season the farm has its best harvest ever.

Leading from

Any Chair

BEN: A conductor can be easily seduced by the public's extraordinary attention to his unique offering and come to believe that he is personally superior. The near-mythical maestro Herbert von Karajan was reputed to have jumped into a taxi outside the opera house and shouted to the driver, "Hurry, hurry!" "Very good, sir," said the driver. "Where to?" "It doesn't matter," said von Karajan impatiently. "They need me everywhere!"

Orchestral players will forgive a great conductor—one who has a far-reaching artistic vision—many personal transgressions in facilitation of the all-important performance, much the way a family will administer to the extraordinary needs of a woman giving birth. Yet in the music business, as in all walks of life, a leader who feels he is superior is likely to suppress the voices of the very people on whom he must rely to deliver his vision alive and kicking.

The conductor, a magical figure for the audience, enjoys a leadership mystique of significant magnitude. It may seem strange

to the orchestral musician that the corporate world would be interested in hearing a conductor's views on leadership or that the
metaphor of the orchestra is so frequently used in the literature of
leadership because, in fact, the profession of conductor is one of
the last bastions of totalitarianism in the civilized world!

There is a famous tale of Toscanini, the great Italian maestro,
whose temper and blatantly autocratic ways—as much as his transcendent musicianship—were the stuff of legend. It is said that
once in the middle of a rehearsal, in a fit of anger, he fired a long-
standing member of the double bass section, who now had to return
home to tell his wife that he was out of a job. As the bass player
packed up his instrument, he mentioned a few things that he had
hitherto kept to himself, and, as he left the hall for the final time,
shouted at Toscanini, "You are a no-good son-of-a-bitch!" So oblivi-
ous was Toscanini to the notion that a player would dare to challenge his authority, that he roared back: "It is too late to apologize!"

This kind of domination of the orchestra by the conductor—
widespread, if not the norm, fifty years ago—is less common today.
But vanity and tyranny are prevalent in the music world even in
these enlightened times, and the picture of orchestral musicians as
infantile and submissive, caught between willful conductors,
insensitive management, and hypervigilant unions, is not as rare as
one would hope. Perhaps that is part of the reason why a recent
study of various professions revealed that orchestral players, while
not the *most* disaffected in the survey, experience a job satisfaction
level just below that of prison guards.[1]

THE SILENT CONDUCTOR

I had been conducting for nearly twenty years when it suddenly
dawned on me that the conductor of an orchestra does not make a
sound. His picture may appear on the cover of the CD in various
dramatic poses, but his true power derives from his ability to make

---

[1] Paul R. Judy, "Life and Work in Symphony Orchestras: An Interview with J. Richard Hackman,"
   Harmony: Forum of the Symphony Orchestra Institute, vol. 2 (April 1996), 4.

other people powerful. I began to ask myself questions like "What makes a group lively and engaged?" instead of "How good am I?" So palpable was the difference in my approach to conducting as a result of this "silent conductor" insight, that players in the orchestra started asking me, "What happened to you?" Before that, my main concerns had been whether my interpretation was being appreciated by the audience and, if the truth be known, whether the critics liked it because if they did it might lead to other opportunities and greater success. In order to realize my interpretation of the work in question, it seemed all I had to do was to gain sway over the players, teach them my interpretation, and make them fulfill my musical will. Now, in the light of my "discovery," I began to shift my attention to how effective I was at enabling the musicians to play each phrase as beautifully as they were capable. This concern had rarely surfaced when my position appeared to give me absolute power and I had cast the players as mere instruments of my will.

But how, actually, could I know what the players were feeling about my effectiveness in releasing their power? Certainly I could tell a lot by looking into their eyes—the eyes never lie, after all—and at their posture, their whole demeanor, and I could ask myself, "Are they engaged?" But at some point, I found I wanted more information, and more relationship. Our eyes meeting across a crowded room was simply not enough; I wanted to hear what they had to say. It was completely impractical to attempt to be on speaking terms with a hundred players at every rehearsal, however, and anyway, there was no precedent for it. Traditionally, all verbal communication in an orchestral rehearsal is directed from the podium to the players and almost never the other way around. Any communication back to the conductor is through a few leading players, especially the concertmaster, and then almost invariably in the form of a question, usually preceded by a semi-diffident, often secretly mocking, "Maestro. . . ."

"Virtually every communication from the musicians to a conductor in a rehearsal is phrased as a question, even when it is really a statement of fact or belief," wrote Seymour and Robert Levine in an article in *Harmony* magazine.

One of [us] once heard the principal clarinetist of a major American orchestra ask the conductor whether he wanted the notes with dots over them ". . . short, or like the brass were playing them?" [A dot over a note indicates that it is to be played short.] This rather complex statement, masquerading as a question, conveyed both the musician's lack of respect for the brass players in question, and scorn for the conductor's failure to notice the problem. But to fit the myth of the omniscient conductor, the comment had to be phrased as a question, for how could a musician possibly inform an omniscient being? The myth dictates that a musician can only tap into that well of knowledge, not add to it.[2]

One time, as we were rehearsing Mahler's Sixth Symphony, I made a seemingly routine apology to the players of the Philharmonia Orchestra of London. You see, I had shouted out after one passage, "Cowbells, you didn't come in!" A few minutes later I realized that the cowbells weren't supposed to play at that moment, so I called out to the percussion section, "I'm so sorry, I was wrong about that entrance. I realize you don't play there." After the rehearsal, I was amazed that no less than three musicians came to me separately and in private to say that they couldn't remember the last time they had heard a conductor admit his own mistake. One player commented on how dispiriting it is for players when a conductor, as often happens, gets angry and blames the orchestra when he himself made the mistake, in the vain hope that nobody will have noticed. Many corporate heads and managers I have spoken to have since let me know that the orchestra is not the *only* hierarchical setting where this dynamic occurs.

WHITE SHEETS

With the intention of providing a conduit for orchestra members to be heard, I initiated a practice of putting a blank sheet of paper on

[2] Seymour Levine and Robert Levine, "Why They Are Not Smiling," *Harmony* vol. 2 (April 1996): 18.

every stand in each rehearsal. The players are invited to write down any observation or coaching for me that might enable me to empower them to play the music more beautifully. At first I braced myself for criticism, but surprisingly the responses on the "white sheets," as they have come to be called, rarely assume that form.

Initially, out of habit, players confined their remarks to practical issues, such as the agreement between the parts and the score. Gradually, when they trusted that I was genuinely interested in what they had to say, they began to support me, not by bolstering my authority, nor my ego, but by giving recognition to my role as an essential conduit for the full realization of the possibility of the music. Now that the "white sheet" practice is familiar and accepted by all the orchestras that I regularly conduct, the comments, which are usually signed to facilitate further discussion, are most often practical ones about my conducting or about the interpretation of the music. Musicians do not hesitate to ask me, for instance, to conduct a certain passage in two rather than in four, so they can better fulfill the sense of the musical line.

Frequently I receive comments that are deeply insightful about the interpretation, comments that I almost always take on board and that affect the performance. An orchestra of a hundred musicians will invariably contain great artists, some with an intimate or specialized knowledge of the work being performed, others with insight about the tempo or structure or relationships within the piece, a subject about which no one has ever asked them to communicate.

Whenever I take on an idea from a member of the orchestra, I try to make some eye contact with them at the moment the passage is played, sometimes several times during the rehearsals and even at the concert. Magically, that moment becomes *their* moment. *"You did my crescendo!"* said a cellist with a mixture of disbelief, pride, and delight after the concert; she had written on her white sheet only that morning at the dress rehearsal that we weren't doing justice to one of Bruckner's majestic climaxes.

One of the most supremely gifted and accomplished artists I have known sat for decades as a modest member of the viola section of one of America's leading orchestras. Eugene Lehner had been the violist of the legendary Kolisch Quartet, and had coached the distinguished Julliard String Quartet as well as innumerable other ensembles. Many of Boston's finest musicians considered Lehner to be a seminal, formative influence on their musical lives. How often I have consulted him on thorny points of interpretation—to have the scales removed from my eyes by his incandescent insight into the music!

Yet, had any conductor visiting the Boston Symphony ever consulted him or called on his profound knowledge and understanding of the particular piece they were performing together? Indeed, I believe such a notion is almost unthinkable. One Friday, when he was a guest coach at my Interpretation class, I raised this issue; for the benefit of the class I asked him, "How can you bear to play day after day in an orchestra led by conductors, many of whom must know so much less than you?" In his habitual humility, he sidestepped the compliment and then indicated that he did indeed have something to say on the subject:

> One day, during my very first year playing with the orchestra, I remember an occasion when Koussevitsky was conducting a Bach piece and he seemed to be having some difficulty getting the results he wanted—it simply wasn't going right. Fortunately, his friend, the great French pedagogue and conductor Nadia Boulanger, happened to be in town and sitting in on the rehearsal, so Koussevitsky took the opportunity to extricate himself from an awkward and embarrassing situation by calling out to her, "Nadia, please, will you come up here and conduct? I want to go to the back of the hall to see how it sounds." Mademoiselle Boulanger stepped up, made a few comments to the musicians, and conducted the orchestra through the passage without a hitch. Ever since that time, in every rehearsal, I have been waiting for the conductor to say, "Lehner, you come up here and conduct, I want to go to the back of the hall to hear how it sounds." It is now forty-three years since this happened, and it is less and less likely that I will be asked. However, in the meantime, I haven't had a single dull moment in a rehearsal, as I sit wondering what I would say to the orchestra should I suddenly be called upon to lead.

During a recent stint guest-conducting the orchestra at the Royal College of Music in London, I told, as I often do, the story of Lehner, as a way of encouraging the greatest possible attentiveness and participation of all the players. Then, in the middle of the rehearsal, I suddenly turned to one of the violinists sitting in the fourth stand of the second violins, whose passion had been evident to me from the very first rehearsal, and said, "John, you come up here and conduct. I want to go to the back to hear how it sounds." That day on his white sheet he wrote that I had enabled him to realize a lifelong dream. Suddenly, the full extent of the resources of the orchestra presented itself to my view, and I leapt to offer some of the other musicians the same gift. One wrote, *"I have been so critical of conductors, and now I see that what you have to do is as demanding as playing an instrument."* Others commented that this exercise shifted the whole experience of playing in an orchestra from a passive one to one in which, like Lehner, they became active participants.

How Much Greatness Are We Willing to Grant ?

The conductor decides who is playing in his orchestra. Even when he comes in fresh to guest-conduct players who are already in their seats, he determines who is there. When he sees instrumentalists who look listless, he can decide that they are bored and resigned, or he can greet in them the original spark that enticed them into music, now dimmed to a flicker. He can say, "Of course! They have had to go against their passionate natures and interrupt the long line of their commitment on account of the many competing demands of the music profession. They want to be recognized as the true artists they really are." He can see, sitting before him, the jaded and the disaffected—or the tender and ardent lover of music.

A monumental question for leaders in any organization to consider is: How much greatness are we willing to grant people? Because it makes all the difference at every level who it is we decide we are leading. The activity of leadership is not limited to conductors, presidents, and CEOs, of course—the player who energizes the orchestra by communicating his newfound appreciation for the tasks of the conductor, or a parent who fashions in her own mind that her children desire to contribute, is exercising leadership of the most profound kind.

LISTENING FOR PASSION and commitment is the practice of *the silent conductor* whether the players are sitting in the orchestra, on the management team, or on the nursery floor. How can this leader know how well he is fulfilling his intention? He can look in the eyes of the players and prepare to ask himself, "Who am *I* being that they are not shining?" He can invite information and expression. He can speak to their passion. He can look for an opportunity to hand them the baton.

> *Today was exceptional in that I learned leadership is not a responsibility—nobody has to lead. It's a gift, shining silver, that reminds people huddled nearby why each shimmering moment matters. It's in the eyes, the voice, this swelling song that warms up from the toes and tingles with endless possibilities. Things change when you care enough to grab whatever you love, and give it everything.*
>
> —Amanda Burr, student at the Walnut Hill School

LEADERS EVERYWHERE

BEN: On our 1999 tour to Cuba with the Youth Philharmonic Orchestra, we decided to begin a concert in Havana with two pieces to be performed in combination with the National Youth Orchestra of Cuba, a Cuban and an American sitting at each stand. The first piece to be played was written by the outstanding conductor of the Cuban orchestra. It was colorful and brilliant, and contained many complicated Cuban rhythms. I had decided not to prepare our orchestra in advance because I thought it was a rare opportunity to start work on a piece under the direction of the composer himself.

Maestro Guido Lopez Gavillan began rehearsing his work, but it soon seemed evident that the complex Cuban rhythms were so unfamiliar to the American kids that the piece was beyond them. They simply couldn't play it. The maestro became concerned, frustrated, and then resigned himself to failure. He declared from the podium, "I'm afraid this is not going to work. We have to cancel the performance."

This outcome was completely unacceptable to me. It was one of the cornerstones of this trip that our young musicians be able to perform with their counterparts. Without thinking, I leapt to the stage and said to the young Cuban players through an interpreter, "Your job is to teach these rhythms to your stand partner." And to the American players I said, "Just give yourselves over to the leaders sitting next to you. You will get the support you need." I asked the maestro to try again.

What happened next startled us all. The focus shifted away from the maestro, toward the stand partners. Already more expressive than most young players I had seen, the Cubans became fantastically energized, exuberantly conducting with their instruments, each leading along his American stand partner enthusiastically. The American kids, basking in the lavish attention, gave themselves over to the process and began to play the rhythms the way they were intended to be played. Maestro Gavillan, who appeared as surprised and as pleased as I was, nodded to me that everything would be fine.

Then it was my turn, and I rose to conduct the other piece that was to open the program: Bernstein's fiendishly difficult little masterpiece, his overture to *Candide*. This piece was so tricky to play that we had sent the parts down to Havana three months earlier to make sure that the Cuban orchestra would have the opportunity to prepare. As we were getting ready to rehearse, I asked their leader in passing whether they had enjoyed working on the overture. "But we've never seen it," he said, obviously perplexed. It turned out that the music had been languishing in the Cuban post office for all that time.

I could feel the blood drain from my face. I felt panic over-coming me, realizing the impossibility of performing *this* piece under *these* conditions. Our youth orchestra had taken months to master the overture! Then, I looked at the players and saw many of them smiling. Of course! We had only to reverse the process that had been so successful earlier in the rehearsal! The American kids now sprang to life, energetically leading their stand partners through the bar lines—and it went off perfectly. Again, the atten-tion shifted away from the conductor on the podium to the part-nership in the pit. The energy level of each local "conductor" rose dramatically. No less remarkable was the willingness of the young Cuban players to be supported and led by their close compan-ions—and how much more effectively than by the distant figure on the podium.

LIKE LEHNER'S TALE, the story of these young people high-lights another meaning of the phrase *silent conductor*. A leader does not need a podium; she can be sitting quietly on the edge of any chair, listening passionately and with commitment, fully pre-pared to take up the baton. In fact, to make reference to the Rabbi's gift at the end of chapter 3, the leader may be any one of us.

Mr. Zander,

This is my first white sheet. Sitting at the back of the cello sec-tion, when I have always sat at the front, was the hardest thing I've done in a long while. But over the nine days of our work together I began to discover what playing in an orchestra was really about. Your shine has inspired me to believe that I have the force of personality to power the section from wherever I sit and I believe that I led that concert from the 11th chair. Thank you for helping me know that. From this day I will be leading every section in which I sit—whichever seat.

—*Georgina, cellist in the*
New Zealand National Youth Orchestra

Here is a final story of a committed and passionate man, a colleague of Eugene Lehner's, who led as a peer from the edge of his chair with so little fanfare that no one actually noticed him. They just heard the remarkable result.

The legendary Kolisch Quartet had the singular distinction of playing its entire repertoire from memory, including the impossibly complex modern works of Schoenberg, Webern, Bartok, and Berg. Eugene Lehner was the violist for the quartet in the 1930s. Lehner's stories about their remarkable performances often included a hair-raising moment when one player or another had a memory slip. Although he relished the rapport that developed between them without the encumbrance of a music stand, he admits there was hardly a concert in which some mistake did not mar the performance. The alertness, presence, and attention required of the players in every performance is hard to fathom, but in one concert an event occurred that surpassed their ordinary brinkmanship.

In the middle of the slow movement of Beethoven's String Quartet op. 95, just before his big solo, Lehner suddenly had an inexplicable memory lapse, in a place where his memory had never failed him before. He literally blacked out. But the audience heard Opus 95 as it was meant to be played, the viola solo sounding in all its richness. Even the first violinist, Rudolph Kolisch, and cellist, Bennar Heifetz, both with their eyes closed and deeply absorbed in the music, were unaware that Lehner had dropped out. The second violinist, Felix Khuner, was playing Lehner's melody, coming in without missing a beat at the viola's designated entrance, the notes perfectly in tune and voiced like a viola on an instrument tuned a fifth higher. Lehner was stunned, and offstage after the performance asked Khuner how he could have possibly known to play. Khuner answered with a shrug: "I could see that your finger was poised over the wrong string, so I knew you must have forgotten what came next."

Rule

Number 6

Two prime ministers are sitting in a room discussing affairs of state. Suddenly a man bursts in, apoplectic with fury, shouting and stamping and banging his fist on the desk. The resident prime minister admonishes him: "Peter," he says, "kindly remember Rule Number 6," whereupon Peter is instantly restored to complete calm, apologizes, and withdraws. The politicians return to their conversation, only to be interrupted yet again twenty minutes later by an hysterical woman gesticulating wildly, her hair flying. Again the intruder is greeted with the words: "Marie, please remember Rule Number 6." Complete calm descends once more, and she too withdraws with a bow and an apology. When the scene is repeated for a third time, the visiting prime minister addresses his colleague: "My dear friend, I've seen many things in my life, but never anything as remarkable as this. Would you be willing to share with me the secret of Rule Number 6?" "Very simple," replies the resident prime minister. "Rule Number 6 is 'Don't take yourself so g—damn seriously.'" "Ah," says his visitor, "that is a fine rule." After a moment of pondering, he inquires, "And what, may I ask, are the other rules?"

"There aren't any."

BEN: I am often invited to give talks on leadership in various settings, and in one instance, I told the *Rule Number 6* story to a group of executives at a company in Europe. Several months later, when I returned to that city, I dropped by their headquarters and was invited into the president's office. There I was very surprised to see on the desk a plaque facing toward the president's chair, inscribed with the words, *Remember Rule Number 6.*

The president then informed me that a similar plaque now stood on the desks of every manager in the company, with the inscription facing *both* ways. He said that the climate of cooperation and collegiality that had resulted from this one simple act had transformed the corporate culture.

THE PRACTICE OF this chapter is to *lighten up,* which may well light up those around you.

It is not about telling other people not to take *themselves* so seriously, unless your whole group, like the company above, has voluntarily adopted the practice. But you can tell this joke, or any other, in the midst of a tense situation as an invitation to camaraderie. Humor and laughter are perhaps the best way we can "get over ourselves." Humor can bring us together around our inescapable foibles, confusions, and miscommunications, and especially over the ways in which we find ourselves acting entitled and demanding, or putting other people down, or flying at each other's throats.

Dear Ben,

You've taught me the different roles humor can play in working with people, relaxing, empowering, freshening. I can remember one rehearsal, close to a December concert, when we were trying to prepare Bartok's Concerto for Orchestra for the performance. It was not going well. I think that many of us, including myself, had taken some standardized test earlier that day, in addition to other rehearsals and coachings in the afternoon. I know that I was mentally exhausted, and we all kept missing notes and entrances. "Take it straight through the second movement," you said to us, "and NO MISTAKES." I don't know about anyone else, but all my muscles tensed, and I wanted nothing more than to run away and crawl into a hole. You must have sensed this, because you thought a moment and then said, "If you make a mistake . . . a five-hundred-pound cow will fall on your head." Partly from the image, and partly from the complete surprise of hearing that word out of your mouth, we all began to laugh, and everything was better, including the Bartok. I don't think anything could have relaxed or empowered me more at that moment than the word "cow."

—Kate Bennett, from her final white sheet as a graduating member of the Youth Philharmonic Orchestra

REMEMBERING *Rule Number 6* can help us distinguish (and hold at some remove) the part of ourselves that developed in the competitive environment of the "measurement world." For the sake of discussion, we'll call it our *calculating self*. One of its chief characteristics, as we shall see, is that it lobbies to be taken very seriously indeed. When we practice *Rule Number 6*, we coax this *calculating self* to lighten up, and by doing so we break its hold on us.

THE CALCULATING SELF

This *calculating self* is concerned for its survival in a world of scarcity. Its voice, the voice of Peter or Marie, is a version of the one that announced our arrival here on earth with wails and cries, and then learned to smile coyly or stamp its foot to say, "Take note of me."

A child is an exquisite attention-getting device, designed to sound an alarm at the first indication that he will be forgotten or relegated to a position where he does not count. He needs the care and attention of strong, competent people to make it through, and nature obliges by endowing him with enough fear and aggression to stimulate him to hold on fiercely to sources of viability. His education in the ways of relationship sets him the primary task of understanding hierarchy, assessing where the power is, and learning what he must do to be accepted. A child's ability to control his position and the attention of others is critical, much more important than control is for the average adult on an average day.

Frank Sulloway, a former research scholar at the Massachusetts Institute of Technology in the Department of Brain and Cognitive Sciences, suggests that we think of "personality" as a strategy for "getting out of childhood alive."[1] Each child in a family stakes out her own territory of attention and importance by developing certain aspects of her character into "winning ways." One child may be sociable and outgoing, another may be quiet and thoughtful, but both are aimed at the same thing: to find a safe and identifiable niche in the family and the community and to position themselves to survive. Anxiety regulates behavior and alerts the child to the dangers of being one-down, unattended to, or at a loss.

The survival mechanisms of the child have a great deal in common with those of the young of other species, save for the fact that children learn to *know themselves*. They grow up in a medium of language and have a long, long time to think. A child comes to think of himself as the personality he gets recognition for or, in other words, as the set of patterns of action and habits of thought that get him out of childhood in one piece. That set, raised to adulthood, is what we are calling the *calculating self*. The prolonged nature of human childhood may contribute to the persistence of these habits long after their usefulness has passed.

---

[1] Frank Sulloway, *Born to Rebel* (New York: Pantheon Books, 1996), 353.

No matter how confident or well-positioned this adult self appears, underneath the surface it is weak and sees itself as marginal, at risk for losing everything. The alertness to position that was adaptive at an earlier time in an individual's life—and in the history of our species—is still *conceptually* operative in later years and keeps signaling to the self that it must try to climb higher, get more control, displace others, and find a way *in*. Fortunately, the perception of what "in" is, and where it is located, is likely to vary between individuals and groups. Long after any real vestiges of childhood threats remain, this built-in alarm system exaggerates danger in order to insure its life.

We portray the *calculating self* as a ladder with a downward spiral. The ladder refers to the worldview that life is about making progress, striving for success, and positioning oneself in the hierarchy. The downward spiral represents, among other things, the slippage that occurs when we try to control people and circumstances to give ourselves a boost. When this leads to conflict, we are likely to think that we have run up against difficult people and have learned an important lesson. We become more hard-headed and practical. Inevitably our relationships spiral downward. As the *calculating self* tumbles out of control, it intensifies its efforts to climb back up and get in charge, and the cycle goes round and round.

How do we learn to recognize the often-charming, always-scheming, sometimes-anxious, frequently conniving *calculating self*? One good way is to ask ourselves,

What would have to change for me to be completely fulfilled?

The answer to this question will clue us in to the conditions our *calculating self* finds threatening or even intolerable, and we may see that our zeal to bring about change may benefit from a lighter touch. The intolerable condition may be a place or a situation, but very often it is another person.

THE BEST SEX EVER

ROZ: For several years I have been running an "accomplishment program," where people meet regularly in groups for coaching on the completion of individual projects. The nature of these projects can vary widely, from starting a business, to designing a complex Web site, to working through a difficult relationship. But the intent of the accomplishment program is larger than the achievement of specific goals. It is about living life in the realm of possibility.

Over the course of each week, the participants define and follow through on three steps that will take them toward their goals. They can adjust the steps to any size as they go along, so it is virtually impossible to fail. In addition, the whole group is invited to play a common game designed to awaken creativity and highlight the obstructive nature of the *calculating self*. People often discover that the lessons they learn while playing the games are the very tools they use to make their projects, and their lives, leap ahead.

One game I frequently assign comes in the form of *"Have the Best _____ Ever."* This is to encourage people to create an experience that is extraordinarily satisfying regardless of the circumstances around them. So, for example, if the game is *"Have the Best Meal Ever,"* it does *not* say to eat a lot, or to go to an expensive restaurant. It does not say "Do the things that you think are the most likely to get you to your goal." The instructions say, *"Have* it. *Be* fulfilled." Often, that means becoming aware of the fears, opinions, and positions your *calculating self* has adopted that stand in the way of simple fulfillment. If you can remember *Rule Number 6* during the game, you may have a straighter run at ventures that will really make a difference in your life.

I presented this game to one of the accomplishment groups after we had been working together for several months, and I gave them the choice, collectively, to fill out the phrase, so they could set the ante for themselves. Together they decided that "sex" was the only word in the entire English language worth putting in the blank. So, *"Have the Best Sex Ever"* became the game of the week.

One member of the group was not happy about the choice, although she went along with the others. June had left her husband, Mark, earlier in the year after a long struggle to change him. She had found it necessary to erect strong boundaries between herself and this charismatic, energetic, and self-absorbed man, and she wasn't about to back down. "Mark's not going to change," she kept telling us, but it was *she* we were interested in. We reminded her that she could interpret the instructions any way she wanted. In the absence of an intimate partner, perhaps a metaphorical interpretation of "sex" was a way to move ahead. After all, the instructions said, *"Have the Best Sex Ever,"* not, "Have a miserable time against your will with a raging narcissist."

June was meticulous enough about her participation in the group to want to give the game a try, though none of us had a clue as to how she would proceed. What would she discover about herself? We had learned to trust the mysterious power of play.

And, of course, I wouldn't be telling this tale if June hadn't appeared the next week looking radiant. This is her story:

June went on a three-day business retreat and, as is the practice in our group, gave another member, Ann, permission to coach her by telephone as she tackled the assignment. Ann was warming to the game in her relationship with Joe, while June described herself as a royal pain, protesting that the instruction to *"Have the Best Sex Ever"* was both immoral and entirely unsuitable for a woman in her position.

"But Ann kept reminding me that our agreement was at the very least to give the game a try, whether we were successful or not. I hadn't yet imagined who would be my partner, because I thought my husband was the last man on earth I would go near. But I was shocked to discover that as soon as I really let myself think about it, I knew he would be the one."

The group got very quiet, as though any careless gesture would topple this fragile construction.

"And then I remembered *Rule Number 6* and I asked myself, 'What would have to change to make this possible?' And, of course, I came up with the usual answer that *he* would have to change, *he* would have to stop being so self-centered." June looked around, with a mischievous smile, "We're all in agreement, aren't we, that Mark has a narcissistic personality disorder, and will never change?" No one knew what to say. June laughed.

I realized I had been taking myself pretty goldarn seriously. "Why can't you have the Best Sex Ever with a self-centered guy?" I said to myself. "Lighten up."

It was strange. Suddenly Mark's self-absorption got disentangled from the idea of making love. I realized that I'd always been enormously attracted to guys who are self-absorbed and passionate about what they do. I had this sense, in that fraction of a moment, that it was possible . . . making love, fully making love with such a man was of course possible. After all, it had been once. This realization in itself was so interesting, so new, that for a moment I felt daring enough to go to a pay phone . . .

I called him, and this was very difficult because it was like saying I was wrong and he was right. My pride kept flaring up, I felt very nervous, and a little crazy because I didn't recognize myself. I was hoping he wouldn't be home, but of course he was. And it turned out that it was easy to talk to him, even though we hadn't spoken for quite a while. I told him about the game. And after an awkward silence, I added the other half of the invitation. "I do think it would be a good idea if we made love."

He was so quiet that I got frightened the other way. I didn't want to be rejected. And then he said, "This call must have taken a lot of courage to make."

I was at a loss for words. Where had this sensitivity come from, this empathy—in my self-centered mate? We agreed to have dinner at his place on Friday when I returned.

And then things began to change . . . I remember walking down a country road and being aware of everything . . . the

smell of the grass, the shape of the riverbank . . . everything was
sensual; it was as though nature was conspiring with the game.
On the way into town I stopped at a fruit stand to buy dessert,
and my eye was caught by flowers in a pail. I found myself arriv-
ing at the house Friday night carrying flowers in my hand!
Through all my nervousness I had to laugh. Here I was, a once-
decisive woman who had had the courage of her convictions to
leave her husband—a man beyond repair—now bringing flow-
ers to the scoundrel's door. What a drama! Then we were both
laughing and throwing caution to the winds. The evening we
spent together was like a week's vacation, but it was also like
coming home.

We all looked at each other in disbelief. June had become so
much more expressive, so much more *human* than we had ever
seen her. Soon came the inevitable question. Someone asked,
"But isn't it important to make some decisions about people's
behavior, to set boundaries and stand firm for what you believe?"

I answered, "Of course, but do you think that is what June was
doing? I think she was hurt, plain and simple, as Mark overlooked
her time and time again. And instead of revealing her hurt, she
built up a case that Mark was dangerous, although he wasn't a danger in any real sense at all. I think she felt more powerful as the
judge, but the diagnosis she assigned to him stuck, and from there
arose a story of a guy no one in their right mind could tolerate.
When she asked herself, "What would have to change for me to be
completely fulfilled?" June recognized her own *calculating self* in
action. She stopped taking herself and her story so seriously, and
suddenly was able to distinguish her husband from the diagnosis
she had given him."

June added, "You know, I realized after that one amazing
evening I could have walked away from the marriage, and Mark
and I would have stayed the best of friends. I could have said, 'I'd
rather not,' without feeling resigned or embattled. I finally had a
choice."

Bringing Dreams to Newcastle

BEN: One summer I taught a master class at a festival in New-
castle, which was filmed by the BBC. One of the students in the
class was a young tenor who had just landed a job at the prestigious
La Scala Opera Company in Milan and everything about his
demeanor said that we were to take his recent success very seriously indeed.

He was to sing "Spring Dream" ("Frülingstraum"), from Schubert's *Die Winterreise*, a song cycle that describes the yearning
depressive journey of a jilted lover through the cold days of the
soul. In this song, the hero is dreaming of the flowers and meadows
of a springtime past when he delighted in the warm embraces of his
beloved. The gently lilting music conjures up blissful joy, blissful
fulfillment. Suddenly a crow screams from the rooftops—he awak-
ens and discovers it is dark and cold. Half in a dream, he mistakes
the frost patterns on the window for flowers and asks, "Who painted
those flowers there—when will they turn to green?" The answer
comes to him: "When I have my loved one in my arms again." But,
despite the major key, we know from the dynamic markings and
the shape of the phrasing that he will never get her back.

This music is some of the most intimate, soft, subtle, and delicate in the repertoire. It depends for its expression on an understanding of the nuances of sadness, vulnerability, and never-ending
loss. But when Jeffrey began to sing, there was no trace of melancholy. Out poured a glorious stream of rich, resonant, Italianate
sound. Pure Jeffrey, taking himself very seriously. How could I
induce him to look past himself in order to become a conduit for
the expressive passion of the music?

I began by asking him if he was willing to be coached. "Oh, I
love to be coached," he said breezily, though I doubt he had any
idea of what was to follow. For forty-five minutes, I engaged in a
battle royal, not with Jeffrey but with his pride, his vocal training,
his need to look good, and the years of applause he had received
for his extraordinary voice. As each layer was peeled away and he

got closer and closer to the raw vulnerability of Schubert's distraught lover, his voice lost its patina and began to reveal the human soul beneath. His body, too, began to take on a softened and rounded turn. At the final words, "When will I have my lover in my arms again?" Jeffrey's voice, now almost inaudible, seemed to reach us through some other channel than sound. Nobody stirred—the audience, the players, the BBC crew—all of us were unified in silence. Then, finally, tremendous applause.

I thanked Jeffrey publicly for his willingness to give up his pride, his training, and his vocal accomplishment, and explained that our applause was for the sacrifice he had made to bring us to a place of understanding. "Whenever somebody gives up their pride to reveal a truth to others," I told him, "we find it incredibly moving; in fact, we are all so moved that even the cameraman is crying." I hadn't actually looked in the direction of the camera; I was simply expressing my conviction that no one in the room could be left unmoved.

Later that evening, in the pub, the cameraman came up to me and asked how I had known he had been crying. He confessed that he hadn't been able to see through his lens for his tears. "When I was sent on this job from London," he said, shaking his head, "I had no idea that this music shit was about my life."

WHEN ONE PERSON peels away layers of opinion, entitlement, pride, and inflated self-description, others instantly feel the connection. As one person has the grace to practice the secret of *Rule Number 6*, others often follow. Now, with the *calculating self* revealed and humored, the *central self* shines through.

THE CENTRAL SELF

Inscribed on five of the six pillars in the Holocaust Memorial at Quincy Market in Boston are stories that speak of the cruelty and suffering in the camps. The sixth pillar presents a tale of a different sort, about a little girl named Ilse, a childhood friend of Guerda Weissman Kline, in Auschwitz. Guerda remembers that Ilse, who was about six years old at the time, found one morning a single raspberry somewhere in the camp. Ilse carried it all day long in a protected place in her pocket, and in the evening, her eyes shining with happiness, she presented it to her friend Guerda on a leaf. "Imagine a world," writes Guerda, "in which your entire possession is one raspberry, and you give it to your friend."

Such is the nature of the *central self*, a term we use to embrace the remarkably generative, prolific, and creative nature of ourselves and the world.

If we were to design a new voyage to carry us from our endless childhood into the bright realm of possibility, we might want to steer away from a hierarchical environment and aim for the openness and reciprocity of a level playing field—away from a mind-set of scarcity and deficiency and toward an attitude of wholeness and sufficiency. We might even describe human development as the ongoing reconstruction of the *calculating self* toward the rich, free, compassionate, and expressive world of the *central self*.

Resolving Conflict through the Central Self

Since the *calculating self* is designed to look out for Number One, we are apt to find it in the driver's seat wherever people are at an impasse, whether in politics, personal relationships (as in June's story), or in the business world.

The practice of *Rule Number 6* gives the facilitator in a negotiation a unique perspective. For the facilitator versed in this practice, conflict resolution is the art of paving the way for the parties' *central selves* to take charge of the discussion. In other words, the role of the facilitator is to promote human development and transformation rather than to find a solution that satisfies the demands of the ever-present *calculating selves*. In the story that follows, the assumption was made that the two men's *calculating selves* would each be plotting to win out over the other, pulling the conversation into the *downward spiral*, while their *central selves* would know a more direct route to a productive and collaborative solution.

The Inventor and the Money Man

ROZ: Two major partners of a medical research firm were deadlocked over their contract with each other, and every hour was bringing them closer to their financial demise. The younger of the partners, a man in his forties, happened to be sitting next to Ben on a flight from Boston to Dallas, and told him the story. Full of enthusiasm, Ben reached for the phone in the seatback ahead of him and dialed me up. "Oh good, I got you!" he said. "I'm sitting next to a wonderful man who has a problem, and I promised him you could solve it. Here, let me put him on." The next thing I knew Ben had handed the phone to his new friend, and he and I were discussing our next step.

We met at the company's offices at 9:30 the next Monday morning. It was obvious that the senior partner—a man in his early eighties and the company's founder—was *not* happy to see me, and disinclined to submit this in-house matter to a consultant. He was demanding that the junior partner sign a contract agreeing to goals that the younger man thought were impossible to accomplish. The situation had turned into an ultimatum—sign the contract, or get out and lose your investment. No changes, no negotiation, no compromises. The senior partner told me in a dismissive tone that he had an important meeting at eleven o'clock. An hour and a half was all the time he would spend on the matter.

I took as my premise that each man recognized in his heart of hearts the exact way in which he was being adversarial, uncooperative, childish, bent on revenge, and out to save his own skin. At the same time I was pretty sure that each man was feeling entirely justified in such behavior given his partner's actions. In other words, I operated under the assumption that each partner's *central self* knew the workings of his *calculating self*. I intended to speak only to their two *central selves*.

Since it was the younger man who had asked for the consultation, I assumed that he felt he was losing the battle. So, relying on his trust and on the stake he had in the matter, I turned to the senior partner to tell me just what kind of a jerk—I might have used an even more colloquial term—his partner had been. The question was framed to draw out a description of the younger man's *calculating self* in action, so we could see all the ways that the older man felt obstructed. The colloquial appellation I used was intended to indicate, however, that in line with *Rule Number 6*, this behavior was not to be taken too seriously.

And it poured out, how the younger partner had repeatedly promised and failed to raise a certain amount of money, how devious he had been, how he had falsified and shifted his story to suit his own needs. The senior partner suspected him of double-dealing, and he feared that his life's work, his research on the product, was about to go down the drain because, so far, they lacked the funds to manufacture it in time to beat the competition to the market. It was a survival issue for the older man, because he identified himself so completely with the product of his labors.

Of course the younger man protested that these allegations were all untrue, and with each word he sent the senior partner into a fit of renewed exasperation.

In order to identify the primary issue blocking the older man's cooperation, I asked him what irritated him *most* in his dealings with his partner. He gave me a straight answer, "That he lies to himself and to me." I seized the opening to establish agreement between them about what had actually happened.

"Have you raised the money you said you would?" I asked the junior partner. He started to explain, and I stopped him.

"Yes or no?"

"No, but—"

"Look," I said, "I have no doubt that you have all sorts of plans lined up, and that the money may be about to flow in. I don't have any judgment about this. I only want to ascertain whether the money is in the bank now."

"No."

"So on the surface, your partner, a man whose work you respect enormously, has reason to be apprehensive." I was leaning toward him and speaking directly and intimately to the *central self* of the younger man. "This is his life's work. He does not want it to disappear."

"Yes, I know."

A common truth was told. The storm of combative energy subsided.

The next thing I wanted to find out was whether the *central self* of the older man thought it was best for the company that the junior partner stay or go. The *central self* always appraises the truth of the whole situation without guile or agenda.

"Is your partner capable of raising the necessary money?" I asked him.

"Yes," was the answer, "if he would only stop lying to himself."

We had a deal in the making, I was certain now, since both men wanted to see the business succeed, and each felt the other was capable of doing his part.

My assumption was that both aspects of the senior partner, his collaborative *central self* and his strategic *calculating self*, had had a hand in writing the contract. The task was to separate the voices so that the older man would have a choice to draft a more effective document.

I asked him whether he had any sons—had he ever become exasperated enough with their teenage arrogance to secretly hope they would fail? He replied that his sons had never caused him any trouble comparable to the headaches this man had given him. Could he perhaps understand that sometimes a person's good will is so challenged that a part of him (the *calculating self*) wants to

see the other person stumble and fall? He nodded. I asked him if
that part of him had had a hand in writing the contract.

"Probably."

"My guess is that you know precisely what your friend here can
accomplish under the best of circumstances, and what he can't. So
you know that if the part of you that is angered and wants to see
him fail prevails, he *will* fail, and of course the business will go
with him."

He nodded, then curtly complimented his partner on having
hired me.

My sense was that the younger man would now be in a more
cooperative place, because he had witnessed the senior partner virtually admitting to sabotage. When you look to people's *central
selves* and conduct an honest conversation, a culture forms that is
hard to resist. For the *calculating self* to emerge in this culture is as
difficult as trying to hum a tune in B minor while the chorus
around you is singing in C major.

Now the idea was that the two men should work together to
modify the contract to provide the greatest possible support for
their joint venture. For that, I asked the senior partner to interview
the junior partner to find out which parts of the contract seemed
unrealistic to him.

When tension arose over any particular item and the *calculating selves* stepped in, I was there to give full existence to the fears.
This is different than allowing the negotiations to be *run* by the
fears. For instance, when the junior partner said, "I feel this is
unfair because you get all the upside here, and I take all the
downside," I reminded him that his senior partner was fearful
because he had much more to lose than money. "Why don't you
make sure that the contract reflects your capabilities," I said, "and
put a little less attention on what will happen if it doesn't work
out?"

The younger man heard my warning not to argue this point
because it would increase his partner's fear. He recognized that his
job was to earn the confidence of his senior partner.

The older man was relieved to have the junior partner's attention diverted from his own survival and toward the work at hand; in turn, he became more flexible in his conditions.

The conversation became increasingly buoyant and energized. Perhaps the light of their original vision for the company began to filter back through. Both men were now using the strategic skills that had been so fine-tuned by their *calculating selves* for a constructive purpose: to design a contract that would permit the business to thrive. So when the junior partner said, "I can't agree to having that much money in hand by the end of November, but I will have a deal in the works by then. The money will be in the bank by January 1," the senior partner had confidence in his prediction.

They managed to write up the terms of the contract in a format that was ready to be reviewed by their lawyers in time for the senior partner to make his eleven o'clock meeting.

"Good," said the founding partner sternly, "we finished on time." I looked up sharply and saw the glint of humor in his eye, and realized that he had absorbed *Rule Number 6*. The younger partner, feigning innocence, joked, "Yes, but why did it take us so long?" Possibility was in the air.

UNLIKE THE *calculating self,* the *central self* is neither a pattern of action nor a set of strategies. It does not need an identity; it is its own pure expression. It is what a person who has survived—and knows it—looks like. The *central self* smiles at the *calculating self's* perceptions, understanding that they are the relics of our ancestry, the necessary illusions of childhood. Fine, if the child thinks there is such a thing as "not belonging," so he can shriek and wail at the first hint of being forgotten at the grocery store. Fine, if he should think that he needs to be stronger or smarter than others to stay alive, so he will exercise mind and body, resist drowning, and get to the food first.

However, the *central self* knows that "not belonging" and "being insufficient" are thoughts both as native to us and as illusory as Santa Claus. It understands that the threatening aspects of what we encounter are often illusions that do not bear taking seriously. It sees that human beings are social animals; we move in a dance with each other, we are all fundamentally immeasurable, we all belong. What freedom! Unencumbered by the obstacles that the *calculating self* tackles daily, the *central self* can listen in innocence for who we are, listen for the whole of it, inquire into what is here. The *calculating self* will never hear the whispers of compassion between people on a busy street, never feel the complex rhythms of our breathing against the swaying of trees and the oscillations of the tide, never attune itself to the long rhythms that give us meaning. Its attention is on its own comparisons and schemes. But the *central self* is open and aware because it need only be the unique voice that it is, an expression that transcends the personality that got it out of childhood alive.

Transformation, for our *central selves*, is a description of the mode through which we move through life. A transformation is a shift in how we experience the world, and these shifts happen continually, often just beyond our notice. As soon as a person sets out on an adventure, or falls in love, or starts a new job, she is likely to find herself feeling and thinking and talking like a new person, curious as to how she could have felt the way she had just days earlier. From the perspective of the *central self*, life moves with fluidity like a constantly varying river, and so do we. Confident that it can deal with whatever comes its way, it sees itself as permeable rather than vulnerable, and stays open to influence, to the new and the unknown. Under no illusion that it can control the movement of the river, it joins rather than resists its bountiful flow.

Vikram Savkar, a friend of ours, told us the story of an experience that had become for him an icon for the openness and generosity of the *central self*. Yet the story he tells depicts his *own* central self emerging into a cooperative universe, inviting us to join him in play.

Last night, I visited one of my old college haunts, a seedy diner located south of the campus. I took a place at the counter next to a man who appeared, on a second look, to be homeless. Before him, meticulously laid out, were three dollar bills and some change, apparently all he had in the world. When the waitress appeared, I ordered a hamburger—but the man put out his hand as if to slow me down. With a grand gesture, he announced, "It's on me. You can have anything you want tonight, and you won't pay a penny. It's all on me." I protested that I could not possibly do that. He was offering me the whole of his worldly possessions, and I certainly could not accept such a gift. But he was determined to have his moment. "You are going to have what you want, and it's on me." He pushed all his money toward the indifferent woman behind the counter.

I was aware of every delicious bite of that hamburger, every sip of coffee. With a mere three dollars and fifty-odd cents, this man had created a humane world brimming over with charity and abundance. This momentary universe teemed with delicious smells from the grill, while voices of happiness emanated from a couple chatting at a booth. And I, I had the deeply satisfying experience of being there while all this took place. I thanked him for everything.

"Oh, no," he said, winking at my last-ditch efforts to find some parity. "The pleasure's all mine."

WHEN WE FOLLOW *Rule Number 6* and lighten up over our childish demands and entitlements, we are instantly transported into a remarkable universe. This new universe is cooperative in nature, and pulls for the realization of all our cooperative desires. For the most part it lies a bit above our heads. Angels can fly there because, as you may have heard, they take themselves lightly. But now with the help of a single rule, so can we.

The Way

Things Are

From the film **Babe:**

The scene: *Christmas day on the farm. The pig, cow, hens, and Ferdinand the duck crowd by the kitchen window, craning their necks to see which unfortunate one of their kind has been chosen to become the main course at dinner. On the platter is Roseanna the duck, dressed with sauce l'orange.*

Duck (Ferdinand): *Why Roseanna? She had such a beautiful nature. I can't take it anymore! It's too much for a duck. It eats away at the soul . . .*

Cow: *The only way to find happiness is to accept that* the way things are *is* the way things are.

Duck: The way things are *stinks!*

THE COW EXPRESSES an oft-repeated philosophy, while the duck, if truth be told, speaks for most of us—not only about *the way things are*, but also about the cow's sanctimonious and resigned attitude toward life. Presumably, the cow will go like a lamb to the slaughter, while the duck will look for means of escape. But what if there is no apparent way out? Will the duck spend what he conceives to be his last days in misery, flapping against the walls of his cage?

The practice in this chapter is an antidote both to the hopeless resignation of the cow and to the spluttering resistance of the duck. It is *to be present to* the way things are, *including our feelings about* the way things are. This practice can help us clarify the next step that will take us in the direction we say we want to go.

The *calculating self* is threatened by such an attempt: "*Why hang around and feel like a sucker?*" it asks.

But the *central self* expands and develops with each new experience:

"*What is here now?*" it asks, and then,

"*What else is here now?*"

Being present to *the way things are* is not the same as *accepting* things as they are in the resigned way of the cow. It doesn't mean you should drown out your negative feelings or pretend you like what you really can't stand. It doesn't mean you should work to achieve some "higher plane of existence" so you can "transcend negativity." It simply means, *being present without resistance*: being present to what is happening *and* present to your reactions, no matter how intense.

Say, for instance, you are on your annual winter vacation in Florida, and rain is pouring down steadily. Surely you won't like it. You came here expecting sun and warmth, rounds of golf, and lots of time on the beach. The question is, can you *be* with the whole thing, the rain and your feelings about the rain? If you cannot, you might spend entire days bracing against the truth, complaining how unfair it is, how nobody warned you about the weather patterns, how the hotel ought to refund your money because the brochure showed sunny skies, how wrong your spouse was not to take your advice to go to the resort in Tucson. You might find yourself railing at the heavens, asking why you, personally, are being punished. You would be stuck—and unable to go on from there.

However, there is another choice: letting the rain *be*, without fighting it. Merely exchanging an *and* for a *but* may do the trick:

We are in Florida for our winter vacation, AND *it's raining. This isn't what we planned; it's very disappointing. If we wanted rain at this time of year, we would have visited our friends in Seattle.* AND, *this is* the way things are.

Presence without resistance: you are now free to turn to the question, "What do we want to do from here?" Then all sorts of pathways begin to appear: the possibility of resting; having the best food, sex, reading, or conversation; going to the movies or walking in the rain; or catching the next flight to Tucson.

Indeed, the capacity to be present to everything that is happening, without resistance, creates possibility. It creates possibility in the same way that, if you are far-sighted, finding your glasses revives your ability to read or remove a splinter from a child's finger. At last you can see. You can leave behind the struggle to come to terms with what is in front of you, and move on.

A DOWNHILL CHALLENGE

ROZ: One year I went alone on a three-day ski trip, with a plan to concentrate entirely on improving my skiing. On my first run down the mountain, I slipped and fell on a patch of ice. From then on I became vigilant, tensing up in resistance whenever I spotted ice, and, unfortunately, there was plenty of it. I was about to abandon the project and come back some other time when *real* skiing was to be had, when suddenly it occurred to me that I had been operating under the assumption that *real* skiing is skiing on snow. I laughed with what Ben often refers to as "cosmic laughter," the laughter that comes from the surprise and delight of seeing the obvious. If I was going to be a New England skier, I had better include ice in my definition of skiing! I redrew the box in my mind, so that now I had it that skiing is skiing on snow *and* ice. As

I started down the next run, my physical self coordinated easily with my new way of thinking. I welcomed the ice. As every skier knows, resistance to ice can take you on quite a painful downward slide, whereas traversing ice as though it is a friendly surface will usually deliver you gracefully to the other side.

MISTAKES CAN BE like ice. If we resist them, we may keep on slipping into a posture of defeat. If we include mistakes in our definition of performance, we are likely to glide through them and appreciate the beauty of the longer run.

MUSIC'S UPHILL GLORY

BEN: I'll never forget my surprise when the first horn player of the Boston Philharmonic came to me after a performance of one of the most taxing of Mahler's symphonies in which he had played a magnificent rendition of the incredibly demanding solo horn part. "I'm so sorry," he said. For a moment I couldn't imagine what he was talking about. I was struck that his whole appearance seemed dejected and apologetic. Finally I registered that what had caused his deflation was the fact that he had flubbed two admittedly very exposed high notes in the course of one of his big solo passages. Perhaps his mistake might have seemed an irritant to some in a recording heard over and over again, but in the context of an impassioned performance lasting nearly ninety minutes, it was hardly significant. In fact, the all-out ardor of his playing that had led to his mistake had been a major contributor to this performance's extraordinary vitality.

The level of playing of the average orchestral player is much higher than it used to be in Mahler's day. So when Mahler wrote difficult passages for particular instruments, like the high-flying "Frère Jacques" tune for solo double bass in the third movement of the First Symphony, he was almost certainly conveying, musically, the sense of vulnerability and risk he saw as an integral part of life. For the orchestra and the conductor, playing Mahler's symphonies means taking huge risks with ensemble, expression, and technique. We will not convey the sense of the music if we are in perfect technical control, so in a sense a very good player has to try harder in these passages than someone for whom they would be a strain, technically. Stravinsky, a composer whom we tend to think of as rather objective and "cool," once turned down a bassoon player because he was *too* good to render the perilous opening to *The Rite of Spring.* This heart-stopping moment, conveying the first crack in the cold grip of the Russian winter, can only be truly represented if the player has to strain every fiber of his technical resources to accomplish it. A bassoon player for whom it was easy would miss the expressive point. And when told by a violinist that a difficult passage in the violin concerto was virtually unplayable, Stravinsky is supposed to have said: "I don't want the sound of someone playing this passage, I want the sound of someone *trying* to play it!"

This attitude is difficult to maintain in our competitive culture where so much attention is given to mistakes and criticism that the voice of the soul is literally interrupted. The risk the music invites us to take becomes a joyous adventure only when we stretch beyond our known capacities, while gladly affirming that we may fail. And if we make a mistake, we can mentally raise our arms and say, "How fascinating!" and reroute our attention to the higher purpose at hand.

SOME DISTINCTIONS

The practice of being with *the way things are* calls upon us to distinguish between our assumptions, our feelings, and the facts — that is, what has happened or what is happening. These are not easy distinctions to make considering the ongoing inventive power of perception. The following are applications of the practice in some contexts where we may have difficulty distinguishing our thoughts and feelings *about* events from the events themselves.

Being with the Way Things Are by Clearing "Shoulds"

When we dislike a situation, we tend to put all our attention on how things *should be* rather than how they are. How many times have we addressed a "should-be" child and found our words quite irrelevant to the child we've got? The stakes really go up when the issue is not rain or a child's whine, but hunger, tyranny, or global warming. When our attention is primarily directed to how wrong things are, we lose our power to act effectively. We may have difficulty understanding the total context, discussing what to do next, or overlooking the people who "should not have done what they did" as we think about a solution.

Being with the Way Things Are by Closing the Exits: Escape, Denial, and Blame

Some feelings are just plain unpleasant, like being too cold or having a stomachache. Others, like grief or anguish or rage, seem so intense they threaten to overwhelm us, and we look for an exit. We resist the feelings, or turn our backs on the situation, or foist the blame and the responsibility onto others. Closing the exits means staying with the feelings, whatever they are. It means letting them run their course, as a storm sweeps overhead showering rain and thunder, only to be followed by clear patches of blue.

Sometimes the capacity to be present without resistance eludes even the most loving parents when their children are troubled. They may not be able to bear their children's pain, stand close enough to comfort them, or even listen to their words. But feelings can be likened to muscles—the more intensively you stay with the exercise, closing the door on escape, the more emotional heavy lifting you can do. Then you become that much more of a player in your field of endeavor.

Being with the Way Things Are by Clearing Judgments

The rain in Florida may be bad for us *and* good for the citrus crop. A canceled flight may wreck our schedule *and* bring us face to face with our future spouse in the airport lounge. A forest fire may seem to destroy an ecosystem in the short term, yet renew it with vigor for the long term. When a splendid osprey eats a beautiful fish, it is neither good nor bad. Or, it's good for the osprey and bad for the fish. Nature makes no judgment. Humans do. And while our willingness to distinguish good and evil may be one of our most enhancing attributes, it is important to realize that "good" and "bad" are categories we impose on the world—they are not of the world itself.

> *A young man goes to see his rabbi. "Rabbi," he asks, "you told us a story—something to do with praise?" The rabbi responds, "Yes, it is thus: when you get some good news, you thank the Lord, and when you get some bad news, you praise the Lord." "Of course," replies the man, "I should have remembered. But Rabbi, how do you actually know which is the good news and which is the bad news?" The rabbi smiles. "You are wise, my son. So just to be on the safe side, always thank the Lord."*

Being with the Way Things Are by Distinguishing Physical from Conceptual Reality

Among all the complexities that keep us from being present to things the way they are, one of the most potent is the confusion between physical reality and abstractions—creations of the mind and tongue. Language is replete with a variety of "things" that have no existence in time and space but seem as real to us as anything we own—"justice," for instance, or "aesthetics," or "zero." Using these concepts, we can accomplish what we could not otherwise. They are tools that allow us to count, to learn from others, to establish guidelines for behavior. They permit us to traffic with the future and the past. It is important to keep in mind, however, that these "things" refer only indirectly to phenomena in the world. What they point to is not made up of matter. These abstractions are purely inventions of language.

The nature of abstractions is that they have a lasting existence exempt from the contingencies of time and place. The oft-heard lament of women in their thirties seeking marriage, "there are no men," does not refer to tonight in Boston. An abstraction, such as *destiny*, that is thought up in a moment of resistance to passing conditions has the power to narrow down our lives. Two stormy Florida vacations can easily be turned into a permanent cloud of bad karma that follows one whenever fun is in the offing, putting a damper on the brightest day. So this part of the practice of being with *the way things are* is to separate our conclusions about events from our description of the events themselves, until possibility opens up.

The Wall

ROZ: A family came to do some work with me at the request of their sixteen-year-old son. Stress in their household had risen to such a level that the normally reticent young man had actually suggested therapy for himself and his parents. The father had then obtained the referral from his medical doctor. During the first visit, the distraught father told me earnestly, "He doesn't communicate with us; he's put up an impenetrable wall that excludes us from his life." How odd for this man to put it in those terms, I thought, given the fact that his son had been the one to initiate the meeting.

Both parents turned toward their son and waited. The boy said nothing. "You see?" said his father, and went on to elaborate the image; the boy had closeted himself, and the father wanted more of something—more information, more contact.

Now, this is such a common way of speaking that its inventive power can easily pass us by unnoticed. The father spoke about a barrier to communication that he said the boy had created, but of course it only appeared when the father called it up. By the alchemy of language, the four people in the room were instantly transfigured into four people and a wall. The more the father described it, the more the wall increased in density, and the more invisible the boy grew behind it. Taking the boy's silence as further evidence of the barrier, the father seemed unaware that he hadn't made any request of his son or addressed him at all. This well-intentioned man did not realize that, by insisting on there being a wall between them, he had built something more solid than if he had taken mortar and brick and erected an unscalable rampart to divide them. Every bit of communication from then on related to the "wall"; every silence was evidence of its enduring presence.

How life-giving a tiny shift in speaking could become. Imagine this conversation: "Are you willing to pretend that there is a wall between us?" the father asks, and, if the boy agrees, they dismantle the wall in play, where it belongs. Perhaps the young man suggests another metaphor, that he feels "invisible" to his parents. Startled, the adults begin to put their attention on the boy-in-the-flesh in the room with them, with whom real relationship can grow. Imagine that the father begins a conversation with, "Son, you're the best thing that ever happened to me," or "Son, what about this whole situation makes you the most angry?" or "Son, I'm about to tell you something I've never told anyone before." The boy looks up at his father, and they have taken their first steps on a journey of possibility.

Abstractions that we *unwittingly* treat as physical reality tend to block us from seeing *the way things are*, and therefore reduce our power to accomplish what we say we want.

DOWNWARD SPIRAL TALK

In the last chapter, we set up a model distinguishing two selves: the *calculating self* and the *central self*. When we are our *calculating selves*, we struggle onward and upward like contestants in an obstacle course, riveting our attention on the "barriers" we see in our way. Strengthening the concept of obstacles with metaphors, we talk about "walls" and "roadblocks," their height and prevalence, and what it will take to overcome them. This is *downward spiral talk*, and it is part and parcel of the effort to climb the ladder and arrive at the top.

The catchphrase *downward spiral talk* stands for a resigned way of speaking that excludes possibility. "The little old ladies who support classical music are all dying out," the conversation goes in *downward spiral* mode. "Our culture has become totally commercialized, and no one wants to fund the arts." "Nowadays school children are only interested in popular music—audiences for classical music are rapidly diminishing; clearly it is a dying art."

Downward spiral talk is based on the fear that we will be stopped in our tracks and fall short in the race, and it is wholly reactive to circumstances, circumstances that appear to be wrong, problematic, and in need of fixing. Every industry or profession has its own version of *downward spiral talk*, as does every relationship. Focusing on the abstraction of scarcity, *downward spiral talk* creates an unassailable story about the limits to what is possible, and tells us compellingly how things are going from bad to worse.

Why does it spiral downward, why do things tend to look more and more hopeless? For the same reason that red Dodge pickups seem to proliferate on the highways as soon as you buy one and that pregnant women appear out of nowhere approximately eight months before your baby is due. The more attention you shine on a particular subject, the more evidence of it will grow. Attention is like light and air and water. Shine attention on obstacles and problems and they multiply lavishly.

The practice of *the way things are* is a reality check on the runaway imagination of the *calculating self*. It's like the world-weary policeman saying, "Just the facts, Ma'am, just the facts." Radiating possibility begins with things as they are and highlights open spaces, the pathways leading out from here.

Then the obstacles are simply *present conditions*—they are merely what has happened or is happening. The father in our story might say, "I have not inquired about my son's life, and he is not volunteering any information," and he would be describing present conditions in the family. He might add: "I am afraid I don't know the right questions to ask, and it irritates me that he doesn't come to me to talk," and he would still be describing *the way things are*. The father would then be able to see the obvious: that sharing something of himself with his son, or asking some interested questions, would be a likely next step toward greater rapport.

So, too, the chairman of the orchestra board might be satisfied with the description, "There were 800 people in attendance for the March 14th concert and 700 for the program on April 10th," without going on to create a trend. For "diminishing audiences," like bogeymen, are never anywhere to be found except in someone's story. You can shake hands, however, with the 700 people who attended the April concert, and while you're at it, pass out fliers and say, "Can't wait to see you at the next event!"

SPEAKING IN POSSIBILITY

Often, the person in the group who articulates the possible is dismissed as a dreamer or as a Pollyanna persisting in a simplistic "glass half-full" kind of optimism. The naysayers pride themselves on their supposed realism. However, it is actually the people who see the glass as "half-empty" who are the ones wedded to a fiction, for "emptiness" and "lack," like the "wall," are abstractions of the mind, whereas "half-full" is a measure of the physical reality under discussion. The so-called optimist, then, is the only one attending to real things, the only one describing a substance that is actually in the glass.

The practice of being with *the way things are* can break the unseen grip of abstractions created as a hedge against danger in a world of survival, and allow us to make conscious distinctions that take us into the realm of possibility—dreams, for instance, and visions. Imagine if we were to faithfully whisper the immortal words of Martin Luther King, Jr., "I have a dream . . . ," as a preface to our every next remark. Speaking in possibility springs from the appreciation that what we say creates a reality; how we define things sets a framework for life to unfold.

A practice of this chapter and of the book as a whole is to distinguish between talk in the *downward spiral* and conversations for possibility. The question one asks is:

Am I speaking from here?

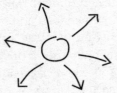

Or from here?

ROZ: "I would do the kind of work that Jane Goodall does, but I couldn't face the horrors she sees everyday," my daughter said as we walked together on a stony beach. Nothing about the moment could have been more perfect: the balmy fragrance of the air, the bright and warming sunlight, seabirds calling from cove to rocky point, while a slight breeze caused the bluest of blues to sparkle with light. It's easy enough to be fully and passionately present on a rare day in Maine, when one is free of obligations and nothing is at stake. But how can we stand to be present in the face of pain, loss, or disappointments?

I had shared with my daughter, Alexandra, my response to hearing Jane Goodall speak at the State of the World Forum in San Francisco. Renowned for her research on chimpanzees in the wild, she has established sanctuaries in Tanzania and in other parts of Africa by working with the people of the areas to support themselves in harmony with the biologically diverse environment. Governments around the world now fund her brainchild, Roots and Shoots, which educates and helps children in at least fifty countries to care for the ecosystem. As she addressed the San Francisco assembly, her quiet speaking captivated the room, as it has so many heads of state. We heard about it all—the poaching, the carnage, the degradations of nature, the destruction of the habitat—but nothing she said stood as a barrier to possibility. Her compassionate gaze encompassed it all, the good and the bad, the painful outrages and the joyous signs of life. Never did she intimate that anything that had happened should have happened differently, not a hint of blame escaped her lips, while she related tales that were torturous for most of us. She simply told the whole story, and showed us the pathways leading out from where we are, while her face expressed only compassion and love. Jane Goodall's transcendent power was rooted in being present, without resistance, to the world just as it is.

BEING WITH *the way things are* calls for an expansion of ourselves. We start from what *is*, not from what *should be*; we encompass contradictions, painful feelings, fears, and imaginings, and—without fleeing, blaming, or attempting correction—we learn to soar, like the far-seeing hawk, over the whole landscape. The practice of being with *the way things are* allows us to alight in a place of openness, where "the truth" readies us for the next step, and the sky opens up.

Giving Way

to Passion

> If I were to wish for anything I should not wish for wealth and power, but for the passionate sense of what can be, for the eye, which, ever young and ardent, sees the possible. Pleasure disappoints, possibility never. And what wine is so sparkling, what so fragrant, what so intoxicating as possibility?
>
> — SØREN KIERKEGAARD, *Either/Or*

ALL AROUND US is vibrancy and energy. The universe is sparking with generative power. But how do we tap into the source—where can we find an electric socket for vitality? Do we have to pump up the energy on our own to carry out the day, or can we catch the current of another wellspring beyond ourselves?

Suppose for a moment that vital, expressive energy flows everywhere, that it is the medium for the existence of life, and that any block to participating in that vitality lies within ourselves. Of course, our minds tell us a different story. The world comes to us sorted into parts: people are distinct entities, shapes have edges, and apples and oranges cannot be compared. Rarely do we come upon or experience this integrative energy, and sometimes only serendipitously, like Alice falling through the rabbit hole. This kind of vibrancy may take us by surprise when we find ourselves committing to doing something extraordinary or when we meet each other on a most personal, elemental level. Yet our minds and bodies are perfectly capable of actively surrendering our boundaries and suspending an edge once we know how and where the lines are drawn.

The practice of this chapter, *giving way to passion*, has two steps:

1. The first step is to notice where you are holding back, and let go. Release those barriers of self that keep you separate and in control, and let the vital energy of passion surge through you, connecting you to all beyond.

2. The second step is to participate wholly. Allow yourself to be a channel to shape the stream of passion into a new expression for the world.

The order and predictability that civilization strives for supports us to get on with the things that matter to us, like starting companies, guiding our children, studying the stars, or composing symphonies. Yet, because the straight-edged organization of our cities and towns—as well as many aspects of our daily lives—tends to mirror our perceptual maps, urban life may magnify the boundaries that keep us in a state of separateness. Places in the wild draw many of us to experience a vitality greater than our own, but it may take an act of surrender to let the gates give way between ourselves and nature.

A LEAP

ROZ: It was late March, and the landscape of northern New England was in a dramatic frame of mind. Skies and mountain lowered in black and white, while dark river water shouldered up under the ice cover. Spring was cracking open and making no bones about it. I walked across a swaying suspension bridge over a formidable section of river, and climbed down the bank on the other side to a focal point of activity. There I faced the scene of an ongoing accident. Titanic triangles of green ice stood straight in the air, as the raving waters split the frozen surface, piling jagged ice sections one upon another. The river roared like mad, its waters roiling by with incessant energy. The abandon was outrageous, confrontational. I could barely hear myself think.

I wavered. It was impossible to be there and resist for long. To preserve myself from this nerve-wracking force, ringing so loudly in my ears, I could have turned away and climbed back up to the thoroughfare, where a roadside diner waited only yards ahead. I could have found a comfortable distance. Yet standing stationary on the bank, utterly still, I took an existential leap. "Let its force run through me," I allowed, not having moved an inch. "Let it turn all my molecules in its direction; trust it and surrender. Let it give me what it has to offer."

And it did, and it has ever since; wherever I seek life's passion, the river is there churning through me. I can hear its mind-numbing rush, the movements of billions of atoms. I see how the ice leapt out of its way, flinging itself upward in sea-colored icons to glory.

Many months later, on a dazzling summer day off New England's coast, I oddly found myself exclaiming, "What is nature asking for?"—not knowing how to cope with so much beauty. I had set off by canoe into secluded coves of dark green waters, where roots of spruce clung to the cliffs' edges with their elbows, grass stems quivered brilliant in the sunshine, and birds darted out over the water. My question, springing from a naive part of me, surprisingly brought forth an answer—"Nature is asking you to feel watery, rock heavy, to reach out with pine branch and leaf. It is calling you to feel the skimming of the water. Participate!" When I began to paint later that day, I found that it was the momentum of nature that showed up on the canvas; not the object, the lines or the color, but dynamic forces, geometric vibrancy, the passion of color.

There is a vitality, a life force, an energy, a quickening that is translated through you into action, and because there is only one of you in all of time, this expression is unique. And if you block it, it will never exist through any other medium and it will be lost. The world will not have it. It is not your business to determine how good it is nor how valuable nor how it compares with other expressions. It is your business to keep it yours clearly and directly, to keep the channel open.

— MARTHA GRAHAM, quoted by Agnes DeMille,
Martha: The Life and Work of Martha Graham

LONG LINES

Like the person who forgets he is related to the waves in the sea or loses continuity with the movement of wind through grass, so does the performer lose his connection to the long line of the music when his attention rests solely on perfecting individual notes and harmonies. Like the person who, mindless that she has all of nature in her fingertips, blocks the expression of the life force, so does the musician interrupt the long line of passion when she limits her focus to the expression of personal emotion, local color, or harmonic events. Her narrow emphasis can produce a dull and numbing performance.

Beethoven's *Moonlight* Sonata is an example of a piece whose meaning changes altogether when a pianist emphasizes the triplets in the right hand at the expense of the long melodic line in the bass, as so often occurs. The tempo slows down to match the interest in the individual somber notes in the right hand, and the character of the piece shifts from the light and forward-looking fantasy Beethoven intended, to a work rendered by tradition as one of deep nostalgia and regret.

Leon Fleischer, the renowned pianist and teacher, has said that playing a piece of music is an exercise in antigravity. The musician's role is to draw the listener's attention over the bar lines—

which are but artificial divisions, having no relevance for the flow of the music—toward a realization of the piece as a whole. In order to make the connections between the larger sections of a piece, the player may find herself moving the tempo at a faster pace than if she were putting her attention on highlighting individual notes or vertical harmonies. This explains how it is that the metronome markings in the works of Beethoven and Schumann appear so fast, indeed *too* fast to many performers and scholars. These composers were passionate about launching a long line.

Life flows when we put our attention on the larger patterns of which we are a part, just as the music soars when a performer distinguishes the notes whose impulse carries the music's structure from those that are purely decorative. Life takes on shape and meaning when a person is able to transcend the barriers of personal survival and become a unique conduit for its vital energy. So too the long line of the music is revealed when the performer connects the structural notes for the ear, like a bird buoyed on an updraft.

BEN: Many years ago, when I was at the conservatory in Florence studying harmony, we were taught to give an identifying rubric to every chord in the music, so that an analysis looked like the ground plan for an office full of separate cubicles. The teachers never suggested that there were any connections between one chord and another, so we remained cut off from the harmonic structure and the flow of the music. We could never get an aerial view of a piece. When one rises above a work to see the long line, the overarching structure, one can see and hear a new meaning, often far beyond the meaning viewed from the ground. And it is only when the essential shape of a musical work is revealed that its true passion can be fully experienced.

A student in my master class at the Walnut Hill School, a preparatory school for the performing arts where I am the artistic director, captured this idea brilliantly on her "white sheet." She

had listened to one of her fellow students perform the first movement of Bach's Suite no. 2 in D Minor for cello, expressively, but
with little sense of the intrinsic shape of the piece. The playing
seemed to wander aimlessly about, pausing here, emphasizing
there, but without a clear notion of the underlying harmonic
motion and melodic line.

After we had analyzed the structure, direction, and character of
the piece in class, the cellist played again with a coherence and
simple flow that had been lacking in her first performance. Here is
what one listener, Amanda Burr, wrote spontaneously, in the few
minutes allotted to the white sheets at the end of the class:

> Whenever I take my glasses off (usually they fall off), I panic.
> For one split moment, the grass becomes green fuzz, the sun, an
> overflowing cup of honey. There's nothing ugly or aggressive
> about nature blurred. But I don't know where I am. I can't rec-
> ognize friends. At any moment I could trip. That's how I felt
> with Hanui's playing—beauty glimmered all around me, but
> nothing was defined. I was helpless in a blur of color. The trans-
> formation Hanui underwent brought clarity, and with it, a
> more intricate, true beauty. The pristine architecture of Bach
> finally rose up to its aching glory.

ONE-BUTTOCK PLAYING

A young pianist was playing a Chopin prelude in my class, and
although we had worked right up to the edge of realizing an overarching concept of the piece, his performance remained earth-
bound. He understood it intellectually, he could have explained it
to someone else, but he was unable to convey the emotional energy
that is the true language of music. Then I noticed something that
proved to be the key: His body was firmly centered in the upright
position. I blurted out, "The trouble is you're a two-buttock player!"
I encouraged him to allow his whole body to flow sideways, urging
him to catch the wave of the music with the shape of his own

body, and suddenly the music took flight. Several in the audience gasped, feeling the emotional dart hit home, as a new distinction was born: the *one-buttock* player. The president of a corporation in Ohio, who was present as a witness, wrote to me: "I was so moved that I went home and transformed my whole company into a *one-buttock* company."

I never did find out what he meant by that, but I have my own ideas. The access to passion gives momentum to efforts to build a business plan, it gives a reason to set up working teams, it gives power to settling individual demands, and it gives urgency to communicating across sections of a company. My fantasy is that this CEO went back and spoke so passionately and so surely to the people in his organization that he straightaway hit the mark — the place of mind, body, and heart. I imagine that his people suddenly remembered why they were there, and what the company was founded *for*. And whenever a person gets bogged down or loses the track, I see that CEO leaning his body toward him, eloquently portraying the whole long soaring line of their future together.

I met Jacqueline Du Pre in the 1950s, when I was twenty and she was fifteen, a gawky English schoolgirl who blossomed into the greatest cellist of her generation. We played the Two Cello Quintet of Schubert together, and I remember her playing was like a tidal wave of intensity and passion. When she was six years old, the story goes, she went into her first competition as a cellist, and she was seen running down the corridor carrying her cello above her head, with a huge grin of excitement on her face. A custodian, noting what he took to be relief on the little girl's face, said, "I see you've just had your chance to perform!" And Jackie answered, excitedly, "No, no, I'm just about to!"

Even at six, Jackie was a conduit for music to pour through. She had the kind of radical confidence about her own highly personal expression that people acquire when they understand that performance is not about getting your act together, but about opening up to the energy of the audience and of the music, and letting it sing in your unique voice.

BTFI

A student from Spain, a member of my Wednesday Sonata and Lieder class at the New England Conservatory, asked me to coach him in preparation for an audition for the position of associate principal cellist of the Barcelona Symphony Orchestra. He played his pieces through with elegance and accuracy. It was playing of an absolutely professional standard, the kind of performance that would, I told him, gain him entry into the ranks of an orchestra. However, it lacked flair and the characteristics of true leadership— not only command of color, intensity, drive, and passion, but the energy to take people beyond where they would normally go. We started work on the pieces—I played the piano, sang, coaxed, and urged him on until his rather formal restraint broke down, and he began to play from the heart and throw all his passion and energy into the soaring passages of the Dvorak Concerto. In the middle of one of his most impassioned utterances, I stopped him and said, "There, that's it. If you play that way, they won't be able to resist you. You will be a compelling force behind which everyone will be inspired to play their best." He wiped the sweat from his brow and from his cello, and we retired to the kitchen for a spaghetti dinner and a bottle of good red wine. As he left the house that night, I shouted behind him, "Remember, Marius, play it the second way!" "I will!" he called back.

Three weeks later he telephoned.

"How did it go, Marius?" I was eager to know.

"Oh," he said, "I didn't make it."

"What happened?" I asked, as I prepared to console him.

He answered matter-of-factly, "I played the first way."

"Never mind, Marius," I said. "You will have other chances." In my mind I vowed to work with him further on releasing his enormous capacity for expression. But it turned out that he had discovered how to break through the gates himself.

"No, no, no," he said. "You haven't heard the whole story. I was so *peesed off*, I said, '*Fock it*, I'm going to Madrid to play the audition for the *principal* cellist in the orchestra there!'—and I won it, at twice the salary of the other job."

"What happened?" I asked again, in amazement.

He laughed. "I played the second way!"

From then on we had another new distinction in the class, called *Beyond the F--- It*, which fast became part of the folklore of all my classes, and showed up in the students as a spiritedness in going beyond where before they might have stopped. Several months after my visit to a Catholic girls' school in California, I received a letter from the headmistress, informing me that *BTFI* had become their unofficial school motto.

Dear Mr. Zander,

I got my A because I am such a special and bright artist. A real artist of human life. The most precious treasure of whole my body is the endless passion of life.

Shu Fen

WE POSE the question again: "Where is the electric socket for possibility, the access to the energy of transformation?" It's just there over the bar line, where the bird soars. We can join it by finding the tempo and lean our bodies to the music; dare to let go of the edges of ourselves . . . *participate!*

Lighting

a Spark

BEN: One of my most vivid childhood memories is of my father, dressed in a three-piece suit, leaving on the overnight train to Glasgow. I asked my mother how long he would be gone, and she assured me I would see him the next evening. "Your father has some things he wants to discuss with a gentleman in Glasgow. They will have breakfast in the Glasgow Railway Station, and then he will take the next train back to London."

"Is it a special friend of his?" I asked, but was told that the gentleman was no one I knew, and someone with whom my father had only a brief acquaintance. This puzzled me. I think I was about eight or nine at the time. Later I asked him why he had not used the telephone. Adopting the stance in which he gave life lessons—eyebrows raised, eyes shining, and, I believe, index finger pointing, my father said, "*Certain things in life are better done in person.*"

This train journey and my father's lesson seemed mysterious and wonderful to me as a child, and took hold in my imagination.

In 1981, when I was asked to lead a tour of the New England Conservatory Symphony Orchestra to the Évian Festival on Lake Geneva, I finally found an application for this long-held memory.

The organizer of the festival suggested that I try to engage the world's greatest cellist, Mstislav Rostropovich, to play the cello concerto that Henri Dutilleux had written specifically for him. As Rostropovich and I were acquaintances, I called his assistant in Washington in October, mentioned the date in April, and asked whether "Slava" would be available. The assistant, with a markedly disdainful air, said, "Are you referring to *this coming* April? Mister Rostropovich is booked all the way through 1984. There is no possible chance he could consider this." I then asked if I might call Slava directly, as I thought his deep love of the music of Henri Dutilleux might prompt his interest. Madame's response was no more pleasant than before, but she finally allowed that Mr. Rostropovich would be in on Wednesday morning at ten, if I wished to telephone him.

In my mind's eye I saw my father, dressed in his three-piece suit, leaving for the train station. Wednesday morning, early, I was at the airport, catching a plane from Boston to Washington. Just before ten o'clock, I walked into Slava's office. His assistant was quite taken aback and visibly irritated, but she announced my presence and showed me into the room where Slava worked. The maestro remembered having given me a cello lesson as part of a master class at Oxford, many years before, and greeted me with his traditional enveloping hug. We settled on the sofa, and began to talk about his beloved friend, the genius composer Henri Dutilleux.

Slava became completely animated, his face shining, as he described the nature of Dutilleux's genius and his unique voice in modern music. Suddenly he asked me when the performance was to take place. I gave him the date. He looked in his diary and said, "I can do it, if it's all right to have just one rehearsal in the afternoon before the concert, though I will have to leave immediately after the concert to make a rehearsal the following morning in

Geneva." This was by no means a rational or practical decision for Slava; it came from his passion. And it involved a huge risk for even a very fine student orchestra to perform an unfamiliar, wildly difficult concerto after just one rehearsal with the soloist. But at least each of us had an accomplice in our folly. I left no more than twenty minutes after I had arrived, murmuring, "He'll do it" to the appalled assistant.

The plane that carried me home from Washington at noon that day was the same one I had taken there, with the same crew in attendance. Recognizing me, a flight attendant asked, "Didn't you just arrive here with us on the eight o'clock?" And I had the pleasure of repeating my father's words: *"Certain things in life are better done in person."* Because I was so excited that Slava had agreed to perform with us, I told the flight attendant the whole story. And, knowing that Slava was the beloved and famous conductor of the National Symphony Orchestra of Washington, the steward announced over the loudspeaker that I had come down to the nation's capital for an hour to entice Rostropovich to play with our New England Conservatory orchestra and Rostropovich had agreed.

The Practice

Enrollment is the practice of this chapter. *Enrolling* is not about forcing, cajoling, tricking, bargaining, pressuring, or guilt-tripping someone into doing something your way. *Enrollment* is the art and practice of generating a spark of possibility for others to share.

In the Middle Ages, when lighting a fire from scratch was an arduous process, people often carried about a metal box containing a smoldering cinder, kept alight throughout the day with little bits of kindling. This meant that a man could light a fire with ease wherever he went, because he always carried the spark.

But our universe is alive with sparks. We have at our fingertips an infinite capacity to light a spark of possibility. Passion, rather than fear, is the igniting force. Abundance, rather than scarcity, is the context. Just as Walter Zander lit a small fire in his young son, so did Ben awaken Rostropovich to a possibility. The maestro carried it further and enrolled Ben in a high-risk venture, which, by the way, turned out magnificently, with Dutilleux, the composer himself, joining the festival in Évian.

So, the practice of *enrollment* is about giving yourself as a possibility to others and being ready, in turn, to catch their spark. It is about playing together as partners in a field of light. And the steps to the practice are:

1. Imagine that people are an invitation for enrollment.

2. Stand ready to participate, willing to be moved and inspired.

3. Offer that which lights you up.

4. Have no doubt that others are eager to catch the spark.

A "no" can so often dampen our fire in the world of the *downward spiral*. It can seem like a permanent, implacable barrier that presents us with limited choices: to attack, to manipulate our way around it, or to bow to it in defeat. In other words, a "no" can seem like a door slamming instead of merely an instance of *the way things are*. Yet, were we to take a "no" less personally, and ourselves less seriously, we might hear something else. We might hear someone saying, "I don't see any new possibility here, so I think I'll stick with my usual way of doing things." We might hear within the word "no" an invitation for enrollment.

The Allegory of the Service Station

ROZ: On an April morning I dusted off my bicycle from its winter hibernation and pedaled toward the Museum of Fine Arts, a route that would take me across the Charles River and along the flowering paths of the Fenway. Finding it hard going over the Boston University Bridge, I stopped to check my tires and saw that the front one was nearly flat. Yet I was in luck, for just ahead, at the foot of the bridge, was a service station whose air pump shone invitingly from across the road. But not up close: it took a couple of quarters to put it into operation, and I, traveling lightly, had only a folded ten-dollar bill in my shirt pocket.

Two big men were in attendance, one at the pumps and one standing idle. I approached them, my ten-dollar bill outstretched. "Do you have change for the air pump?" I asked. They shook their heads. No. It was Sunday, and the till was empty, they explained. I showed them that my tire was flat and that the air pump wouldn't work without two quarters. Again they shook their heads, looking away and down, their hands in their pockets, shuffling their feet like two slow bears.

Three unhappy people, a worthless ten-dollar bill, an air pump standing idle, a bicycle one could not ride, and great art out of reach. "How unnecessary!" I thought. "How irritating, how petty," I argued as I went down in defeat. But nothing changed—there was the idle air pump, the airless tire, the ten-dollar bill that wasn't worth the paper it was printed on, and there we were, we hapless three. . . . With that last thought my perspective lightened, and I felt a shift. I glimpsed, for an instant, that the very people I perceived to be blocking me, their elusive change jingling in their pockets, shared my distress. We were *three* unhappy people.

Then a molecular change, a brightening of the day.

"Will you *give* me two quarters?" I asked, cheerfully, intimately, my whole self on the wing.

The man before me looked up slowly as though confronted with an ancient riddle. The onlooker sprung to life. "Yes!" he said, reaching into his pockets, "I can *give* you the quarters," and he stretched out his hand. And then, suddenly, miraculously, it *all* worked: the coins, the air pump, the bicycle, our partnership. Yet the other gentleman still stood in some confusion. "Do you know a back-roads route to the Museum of Fine Arts?" I asked. He beamed. The directions spilled forth as from a horn of plenty.

Like a tap to a kaleidoscope that shifts identical pieces of glass into different patterns, the scene changed before our eyes from bankruptcy to abundance with just the slightest nudge to the frame. Initially we were relating to each other in the assumption that money is scarce, exchanges must be fair, and that property boundaries were impenetrable. This perspective had us locked into a condition of breakdown. From there I might have cajoled and persuaded them to give me the quarters: "*Look, lend me two quarters for goodness sake, and I'll return the money on the way back from the museum,*" and I might have gotten my dreary way. But it would hardly have brightened anyone's morning.

Not even mine. Persuasion is typically used to get the thing *you* want, whether or not it is at someone else's expense. Persuasion works fine when the other person's agenda matches yours or when the transaction somehow benefits them as well. We call that "aligning interests." But in this case there was nothing in it for the two men, at least from the world of measurement, except to see me on my way.

The practice of *enrollment*, on the other hand, is about generating possibility and lighting its spark in *others*. It is not about the quarters. The sudden realization that we were all trapped in a box of scarcity, unable to act effectively over a matter that cost no more than fifty cents enabled me to step into a universe of possibility — the only place from which you can enroll other people. This may seem like an easy leap, but how often when we are caught behind a driver who has veered into the exact-change lane by mistake do we sit there honking and fuming? Why not jump out of our car and toss two quarters in the bin?

The plain request "Will you give me two quarters?" conveyed a vibrant new world, one in which asking, giving, and receiving were all easy, generous acts. Possibility has its own music, its own gestures, its own kind of radiance, and the attendant caught the spark. How could we help but be joyous that we had the means among us to make everything work?

EASTLEA: A "FAILING" SCHOOL

BEN: I was helping the Philharmonia Orchestra of London land a corporate sponsor for one of our concerts, and I approached Arthur Andersen. They turned us down, citing too many other commitments and not enough staff to handle such an event. I made a quick translation in my mind and concluded that they had not seen a strong possibility in the venture. They were not *enrolled*.

So, when on a subsequent visit I arrived in London and found an invitation to a formal dinner for that very evening from the man who had been in the position of granting or refusing my request, I saw it as an opportunity. However, my suitcase was stranded in Holland, and since I was dressed in jeans and sneakers, I went straight out to Selfridges to buy a complete evening wardrobe.

The dinner conversation turned to the company's involvement in a government-run program to improve a group of schools designated by the Ministry of Education as "failing." As an educator, I am acutely aware that poverty, neglect, and decades of resignation on the part of teachers, families, and administrators can have a devastating effect on children's development. The Newham Project, alias Education Action Zone, was to be launched with the personal involvement of the prime minister the following September. By the end of our dinner, I, who had come to see if I might obtain a sponsorship for my project, found myself fully enrolled in *theirs*. The dim shape of a collective plan began to emerge.

It was suggested that I go to one of the "failing" schools to introduce the students to classical music with the idea that children and teachers alike would come to believe in their own creativity through the metaphor of music. Arthur Andersen would take on the expense of bringing the entire Philharmonia Orchestra to the school for a subsequent session. In addition, they agreed to sponsor two hundred of the students who might choose to attend our concert at the Royal Festival Hall. And, oh yes, in recognition of my participation in this educational initiative, Arthur Andersen offered to fully sponsor the Philharmonia concert.

The Eastlea School is located in the toughest, bleakest section of London's Docklands district, where the pupil population is largely minority. In my initial visit to the school to meet with the administrators, I was surprised to see that all the children were under sixteen. When I asked why this was so, it was explained to me that sixteen is the age at which they are legally able to leave school. Thirty of the children were in wheelchairs with illnesses or congenital conditions as serious as cerebral palsy and spina bifida. Presiding over the whole institution was the irrepressible and indefatigable Maggie Montgomery, headmistress extraordinaire, who enthusiastically welcomed the prospect of the visit of a conductor of some international renown to her school.

We decided on the gym as the only possible location for the first presentation. Maggie admitted that she had never before dared to hold a full school assembly since it would take nearly an hour to seat all eleven hundred students, and their rowdiness was likely to be uncontrollable. She greeted my description of a session two hours long with bemused disbelief, predicting that her teachers would say that fifteen minutes of classical music would be stretching the limit. However, she gave me carte blanche: "Do whatever you think you can do!"

When the day came for my visit, in addition to the kids and teachers, a hundred or so executives and clients from Arthur Andersen swelled the assembled company to over twelve hundred. Television cameras and a crew from the BBC arrived to film the event. This was to be the launching of the Education Action Zone program nationwide.

The *Guardian* newspaper carried an article that very morning with the blazing headline "Education Action Zone May Fail." And that headline seemed all too prescient at more than a few moments during the two-hour presentation. The teachers were doing their best to keep order, but as I looked out over the whole scene, it seemed as though their efforts at discipline were only increasing the tension and noise level. By the end I remember feeling exhausted and thinking the venture really might be hopeless. "I can't subject the Philharmonia Orchestra to this," I thought. The BBC producer saw my spirits flagging and called out, "Ben, you've just conducted eleven hundred kids singing Beethoven's "Ode to Joy" in German! This is a *success!*"

Whatever doubts I had were swept away when Maggie sent me a sheaf of poems the students had written for their English class after my visit. We printed one of them in the Philharmonia program book:

Benz Influence

He came. We laughed, he played. We listened.
   HE CONQUERED!
Vibrant, animated and cheerful, as he swept through
Lifting the schools atmosphere and Confidence. Excitement
Rushing through the whole school (year seven to eleven)
From Mozart to Beethoven. People would think that
Eastenders like us wouldn't have liked it, but as he
Played on his black piano the whole school was
Lifted. He spoke of all the good we could achieve.

Even as an underachieving school. He made me realize that
Education was so important to everyone, not just the
Intelligent, it's as simple as that!

His influence on our school was phenomanal. [sic]
Thanks Ben for helping me and all of
Eastlea Community School.

Karl Kripps, age 14

I also wrote a letter to the children, a copy of which Maggie
gave to each child in the school:

September 21, 1998

Dear Eastlea students,

*I enjoyed our time together and am looking forward to coming
back in less than a month.*

*Do you remember I told you about the headline in the news-
paper on the very first day of the Newham Project, which said in
huge letters: EDUCATION ACTION ZONE MAY FAIL? I
pointed that out as an example of "downward spiral" thinking.
And, sure enough, the day after our session the newspaper carried an article by a woman who had been present and wrote
that she thought it was a pretty hopeless situation; that Arthur
Andersen was wasting its money trying to help schools. "Downward spiraling" is everywhere about us and it is so easy to fall
into the habit of thinking that way.*

*I confess that I too had my doubts, but my assessment of the
situation was quite different: it was the first time the whole
school had been together in the Sports Hall. Getting you all in
was a miracle of organization on the part of your teachers, with
your own good-humored cooperation. You sat quietly for a long
time before it began and then sang, laughed, and listened while
a wild man roamed around on a stage for nearly two hours. At
the end, after you had roared a lusty "Happy Birthday" to Jer-
main, sung Beethoven's Ninth in German, and followed an
analysis of a Chopin prelude, you gave your total attention to a*

piece of music by Mozart played on the piano. WOW! Not bad! I say.

Was it perfect? No! Was it as quiet as it could have been? No! Did I keep everyone's attention all the time? No! HOW FASCINATING! It was a great start!

Now we will soon have a chance to be together again. This time with a full-size symphony orchestra! I am really excited that you will get to hear their sound, and see what happens when I conduct them. I know you will be touched and delighted and amazed!

Will you give some thought to how it will be possible to keep the hall really quiet while the orchestra is playing, so that everybody can enjoy it and the musicians can play their best? I hope that your truly amazing teachers won't feel that they have to work so hard going up and down the aisles keeping discipline. They love music and want to be able to listen too. Do you think it would work to have them sitting down, just listening, like all of you?

Anyway, I am looking forward so much to being together again to explore the music and have you find out more about how it all works. And I think the people at Arthur Andersen are super to make it all possible. Don't you?

See you on the 22nd of October. And meanwhile, see what happens when you give the people around you an A, not as a judgement, but like a gift.

Warmest love from your friend,

Benjamin Zander

THE PHILHARMONIA ADDS ITS VOICE

As the event involving the Philharmonia Orchestra approached, several people at Arthur Andersen worked intensively and enthusiastically on all the arrangements, while I remained in Boston. A new venue was needed to hold the audience of more than twelve hundred, plus an eighty-piece symphony orchestra. Eventually a huge warehouse was located, and forty buses were hired to transport the children. Chairs had to be brought in, a stage and a platform for television cameras built, and lighting and a sound system installed. The company balked when I requested that a twenty-five-foot movie screen be erected behind the stage so that the children could see the interaction between the conductor and the orchestra. The £2,000 price tag was simply too steep on top of all the other costs, which had now escalated beyond anything they had planned for. But I knew that without that view, half the meaning and interest of the event would be lost. I paid for it myself, and raised £10,000 from the Westminster Bank for the filming.

The youngsters greeted my return with wild enthusiasm, assuring me that the first occasion had not been such a failure after all. Several members of the Philharmonia, who had assumed that the children would be inattentive and restless, looked quite perplexed and became genuinely interested in what I could possibly have done the last time to cause this tumultuous reception. The secret was, I believe, that I genuinely wanted to share the music with the children, and I trusted their ability to respond to it and to be partners with me in our whole undertaking. During the two-hour demonstration, the orchestra, our young guests, and I delved into the high drama of Beethoven's *Coriolan* Overture, the tender pathos and tragedy of Tchaikovsky's *Romeo and Juliet,* and Mozart's sparkling Divertimento in D, which he wrote at the age of the oldest children present.

SEVEN VOICES ARE HEARD

But the tour de force was the slow movement of Beethoven's Fifth Symphony. I began by having the Philharmonia's cellos play eight bars of a gently undulating accompanying figure. Turning around to the young people, I asked, "How many of you heard the cellos?" Naturally, everybody raised his hand. Then, repeating the same eight-bar passage, I asked the violas to add their voice, identical in rhythm, just two notes, a "third," above. Again a show of hands revealed that everybody could hear the sound of two voices together. Now I asked the audience to listen to the cellos and violas playing the same eight bars, with the added sound of a bassoon and a clarinet playing intermittent short leaps, one octave apart. Raised hands indicated that hearing four separate voices simultaneously held no difficulty for the Eastlea students.

Returning to the beginning of the passage once more, we added the soulful, somber song of the double basses, easy to detect in the dark lower register. All that remained to add were two voices, the second violins and the first violins. When the second violins entered to play their part, I asked the eager listeners for their remarks. "They are too loud," shouted back a confident youngster. Members of the Philharmonia smiled at the coaching they were receiving from this ten-year-old from London's Docklands.

Once these six voices were revealed in perfect balance, I predicted to the children that the first violins would play too loud, because "they think they're so important!" Sure enough, despite the warning, their entrance blurred the carefully built clarity of the other six voices. The youngsters let them know that all was not well. Goaded by this challenge, the Philharmonia firsts added their running figuration to the texture at an exquisitely delicate dynamic level, and miraculously, all seven voices emerged in clear relief, each one held in effective balance with the other six. The silence in that huge warehouse was profound, as each child strained to hear everything Beethoven had to say.

The final question: "How many of you could hear seven voices?" At least nine hundred hands waved high in the air. "Now wait a minute," I thought to myself, as I looked out over the sea of hands, "who would have predicted this?" But then, who could have predicted any of this—the sponsors, teachers, children, politicians, film crews, musicians—all gathered together to celebrate the indomitability of the human spirit, all highly focused, engaged, and enrolled in the possibility of people succeeding together.

ANTHONY

As we arrived at the last movement of the Fifth Symphony, I offered my baton to a few of the children to try their hand at conducting. The four-square, simple grandeur of the Fifth's triumphant opening in C major can easily be performed without a conductor; so the Philharmonia, I knew, would not be pulled off track by the inexperienced flailing of a child. I soon noticed a hyperactive ten-year-old in the eleventh row, moving his whole body with the powerful rhythm of the music, and I brought him on stage. The unselfconscious reaction to the music he exhibited in his seat did not prepare me for the highly energetic, utterly convincing conducting he displayed on the podium. Astonished looks on the faces of the orchestra players made it evident that they were being led, inspired, and energized by this ten-year-old who had never before seen a symphony orchestra.

For a minute and a half on the podium, this young man was a dynamic artistic force with powerful gestures and an ecstatic countenance. A few moments later, he was a small child again, covering his face in embarrassment as his schoolmates roared and stamped their excited response. Happily, a television camera from a local TV station, trained on the screen behind the stage, caught his image in their lens. And that night, on the ten o'clock news, all of Britain saw Anthony conducting the Philharmonia in the finale of Beethoven's Fifth.

AT THE ROYAL FESTIVAL HALL

The following Wednesday, two hundred Eastlea students, scrubbed and dressed in their finest, arrived early at the Festival Hall for the preconcert talk and the concert itself. Michael Rawlings, president of Pizza Hut in America, whose managers I was to address the following month, had eighty pizzas delivered to the Hall. We all saw a short film of the previous week's performance. Anthony, who had brought his twelve-year-old uncle to the event, watched himself conducting on the TV screen with awe and disbelief.

Now youngsters from Eastlea moved into the hall to hear the preconcert talk. I then spoke for a full fifty minutes, explaining our unusual approach to Beethoven's Fifth Symphony and comparing it with performance traditions. Refreshing the audience's memory of the story, I played parts of Strauss's *Don Quixote* on the piano to show how skillfully the composer had turned the complex and moving tale into music. "Was that the concert, Miss?" Anthony asked his teacher after my presentation, reminding us how unfamiliar to him were all aspects of this venture.

For the concert itself, the two hundred Eastlea students were placed behind the stage in the prominent seats usually occupied by the chorus, so they would be close to the action. I cannot deny that I had been worried that they might fidget and distract the audience, especially since by the time the concert started they had already been in the hall for over two hours. But they sat motionless and apparently riveted throughout Beethoven's Fifth Symphony, as well as through the long and quite taxing tone poem of Strauss. Could we really know what was going on in the minds of those children? Was fear of punishment the true source of their angelic behavior? Were they really listening to the music, or were they being merely dutiful? I stole a glance at Anthony, sitting high on the risers behind the brass section, at the very moment that the shattering burst of light emerges out of the darkness into the glorious sunlight of the last movement of the Fifth. His moment. Would he recognize it? He gave me a big smile and a thumbs-up.

To think that all of this occurred after Arthur Andersen initially turned us down in our request for the sponsorship of a single Philharmonia concert!

In the end, Arthur Andersen's willingness to be fully enrolled in the transformative power of music served to carry the spark to thousands more, including children whose lives might be profoundly influenced by the event. Here is a note I received just before the final concert, from Graham Walker, a senior partner at Arthur Andersen.

Dear Ben,

I know there is the all-important last phase of our trilogy to complete, but I wanted to put something down in writing now. The last phase will take you back to your home territory—the concert hall—so we know that will be a magnificent finale.

The first two phases were on more unfamiliar ground! I was crazy to ask you to participate. You were even crazier to agree. And your infectious enthusiasm immediately caused 70 other grown-up musicians to join us in the crazy zone. Fortunately we found a local authority and head teacher who were crazy enough to play ball. The stage was set, the die was cast and yesterday we all shared the full force of your inspiration, creativity and sensitivity—backed up by the unremitting power of the Philharmonia.

Thank you enormously, Ben. Like you, I hope that these events have set in motion enough radiating possibility to overcome the eddies of gloom that sometimes wash around the lives of our friends in Eastlea. Until Tuesday, and with all our best wishes for your rehearsals—

Graham

THE LIFE FORCE for humankind is, perhaps, nothing more or less than the passionate energy to connect, express, and communicate. *Enrollment* is that life force at work, lighting sparks from person to person, scattering light in all directions. Sometimes the sparks ignite a blaze; sometimes they pass quietly, magically, almost imperceptibly, from one to another to another.

Being

the Board

"That's right, Five, always put the blame on others."

—Lewis Carroll, *Alice in Wonderland*

WHEN *the way things are* seems to offer no possibility; when you are angry and blocked, and, for all your efforts, others refuse to move or cooperate, to compromise, or even to be halfway decent; when even *enrollment* does not work and you are at your wit's end—you can take out this next practice: our graduate course in possibility. In this one, you rename yourself as *the board on which the whole game is being played.* You move the problematic aspect of any circumstance from the outside world inside the boundaries of yourself. With this act you can transform the world.

Imagine this scenario: a car waits peacefully at a red light; another barrels up behind and smashes into its rear. The driver of the second car, it turns out, is intoxicated and unlicensed. Who is at fault? According to the law, there is no doubt: the drunken driver is 100 percent at fault. However, in this chapter, we are introducing the notion of responsibility of a different kind.

This new kind of responsibility is yours for the taking. You cannot assign it to someone else. It is purely an invention, and yet it strengthens you at no one's expense.

Ordinarily we equate accountability with blame and blamelessness, concepts from the world of measurement. When I blame you for something that goes wrong, I seek to establish that I am in the right—and we all know the delicious feeling of satisfaction there. However, inasmuch as I blame you for a miserable vacation or a wall of silence—to that degree, in exactly that proportion, I lose my power. I lose my ability to steer the situation in another direction, to learn from it, or to put us in good relationship with each other. Indeed, I lose any leverage I may have had, because there is nothing I can do about your mistakes—only about mine.

Let's get back to the peaceful, law-abiding driver. To apply the practice of *being the board*, that driver, even from her hospital bed, will cast a wider framework around events than one ordinarily does in the world of fault and blame. She might begin with the thought, "Driving is a hazardous business: Every time I step into a car I am at risk. While usually I can count on other drivers to be awake, aware, and law-abiding, there is always the chance, the *chance*, that one of them may fall asleep, drink too much alcohol, have a sudden seizure, or simply be young, angry, and feeling reckless. When I drive, I take that statistical risk; I own that what happens on the road happens in my sphere of consciousness and choice."

THE PRACTICE: PART ONE

So the first part of the practice is to declare: "I am the framework for everything that happens in my life."

This is perhaps the most radical and elusive of all the practices in this book, and it is also one of the most powerful. Here is another way of saying it:

"If I cannot be present without resistance to the way things are and act effectively, if I feel myself to be wronged, a loser, or a victim, I will tell myself that some assumption I have made is the source of my difficulty."

It is not that this practice offers the *right* choice or the *only* choice. We may want to make sure the intoxicated driver gets his due. We may want sympathy, and we may want revenge. Being derailed from our larger purpose, for a length of time, may be an acceptable option. However, choosing the *being the board* approach opens the possibility of a graceful journey, one that quickly reinstates us on the path we chose before the fateful collision intervened. It allows us to keep on track.

Grace comes from owning the risks we take in a world by and large immune to our control. If you build your house on a floodplain of the Mississippi River, you may be devastated when the waters overflow, and you may rail at the river. However, when you declare yourself an unwilling victim of a known risk, you have postured yourself as a poor loser in a game you chose to play. Out of a sense of self-righteousness, you will have given away your chance to be effective. Perhaps to gain other people's sympathy, you will have traded your own peace of mind.

In the legal sphere, fault and blame play an important role. The law-abiding driver is entitled to sue the perpetrator to cover his losses, however they be construed. But we are talking about access to possibility, not to victory or remuneration. Gracing yourself with responsibility for everything that happens in your life leaves your spirit whole, and leaves you free to choose again.

A HIGH WIRE ACT

BEN: Mendelssohn's Italian Symphony starts off as though the music is making a joyful sprint toward a double handspring that catapults it to the high trapeze. Mendelssohn gives the winds eleven quick steps before the violins make their first energetic somersault, but in one concert, while I was pointing to the winds, a single violinist came in with exuberance and gusto after just five steps! It was the kind of confident violin playing you can't help admiring, but it left us out there in space, no trapeze within our grasp. For the first time in my conducting career, I stopped a performance—in front of more than a thousand people. I smiled to the orchestra, said to myself, *"How fascinating!"* and began the piece again. This time, of course, there was no mishap.

Afterward, someone associated with the orchestra asked me in a hushed voice, *"Would you like to know who came in early in the Mendelssohn?"* Whether it was the slightly conspiratorial nature of the question that put me off, or whether it was that such a question was in disturbing contrast with the spiritedness of the music that we had just performed, I found myself saying, "No" abruptly, and then adding, "I did it."

Not literally, of course. I didn't actually play the violin. But in that moment, in the context of the great music we had just made, it seemed absurd to me to consider handing out blame. It could only divide us, and for what? Certainly that player would never again come in early in the Italian Symphony, nor, perhaps, from this time on, make the mistake of a premature entrance in any performance. And I myself would know to be especially careful in guiding the orchestra through those eleven steps whenever I conducted that passage again. There was absolutely no gain to blaming anyone, and a real cost in terms of the blow to our integrity as a group. Besides, I know full well that every time I step onto a podium, I take a risk that things won't turn out exactly as I anticipate them in my ear—but then, there is no great music-making without such risk taking.

I think, in retrospect, that my "I did it" response represented even more than that—I was saying that I was willing to be responsible for everything that happened in my orchestra. In fact, I felt enormously empowered and *liberated* by doing so.

THE TYPE OF responsibility we are most familiar with is the sort that we apportion to ourselves and others. Dividing obligations helps us keep life organized and manageable, as for example, "*I'll* be responsible for making the kids' lunches, if *you* feed them breakfast," or, "It wasn't all *my* fault that our check bounced; *you* forgot to enter other checks in the ledger." We often use reward and punishment to regulate accountability—the carrot and stick, the bonus at the end of the successful year, the threat of being fired. Approval and disapproval are also strong motivating factors, which rely for their effectiveness on the individual's desire to be included and to do well within the community. Because the model is based on the assumption that life will be under control if everyone plays his part, when things *do* break down, someone or something naturally gets blamed.

Apportioning blame works well enough to keep order in a relatively homogeneous community that boasts commonly accepted values and where everyone is enrolled in playing his part. It appeals to our instinctive sense of fairness. However, its effectiveness is likely to be circumscribed in communities of divergent cultures and widely varied resources. It is at this point, when everything else has failed, that you might find it useful to pull out this new game, the game of *being the board.*

A GAME OF CHESS

We might use the metaphor of a game like chess to describe the difference between the usual measured approach to responsibility and the perspective of the new practice. Normally if you were asked to identify yourself with an aspect of the game, you might point to one of the pieces on the board: you might choose to see yourself as the important king, the wily knight, or the humble pawn. As any one of the pieces, you would understand that your job is to achieve your objective, do well by your team, and help conquer the enemy. Or, you might see yourself as the mastermind, the strategist controlling the movements of your forces in the field.

In our practice, however, you define yourself not as a piece, nor as the strategist, but as *the board itself*, the framework for the game of life around you. Notice we said that you *define* yourself that way, not that you *are* that. If you had the illusion that you really were the cause of the sun rising or of all human suffering, your friends would soon have you carted off in a white van or at least prescribed a large dose of *Rule Number 6* as an interim measure. The purpose of naming yourself as *the board*, or as the context in which life occurs to you, is to give yourself the power to transform your experience of any unwanted condition into one with which you care to live. We said *your experience*, not the condition itself. But of course once you do transform your experience and see things differently, other changes occur.

When you identify yourself as a single chess piece—and by analogy, as an individual in a particular role—you can only react to, complain about, or resist the moves that interrupted your plans. But if you name yourself as *the board itself* you can turn all your attention to what you want to see happen, with none paid to what you need to win or fight or fix.

The action in this graceful game is ongoing integration. One by one, you bring everything you have been resisting into the fold. You, as *the board*, make room for *all* the moves, for the capture of the knight *and* the sacrifice of your bishop, for your good driving *and* the accident, for your miserable childhood *and* the circumstances of your parents' lives, for your need *and* another's refusal. Why? Because that is what is there. It is *the way things are*.

THE PRACTICE: PART TWO

Then, in this game, you take your practice one step further: You ask yourself, in regard to the unwanted circumstances, "Well, how did *this* get on *the board that I am?*" or, "Now, how is it that I have become a context for *that* to occur?" You will begin to see the obvious and then the not-so-obvious contributions of your *calculating self*, or of your history, or of earlier decisions that landed you where you are, feeling like a victim. This reflection may bring forth from you an apology that will knit back together the strands of raveled relationships. And then you will be standing freely and powerfully once again in a universe of possibility.

So, if you are waiting peacefully at a traffic light and get smashed in the rear by a drunken driver, you may ask, after your immediate medical needs are ministered to and the shock and fury die down— "How did *that* event get on the board that I am?" If you are playing this game of *being the board*, you do not say, "Why me?" or "The jerk!" or "This has destroyed my summer!" or "I'm never driving in Boston again!" Instead, you might look around, and say, "It's not *personal* that my car was totaled. It's a certain statistical probability that someone would have been there, waiting at the stoplight." Then you might look into the statistics on drunk drivers and see how many are repeat offenders, and notice that there are some loopholes in the law, which, if closed, might reduce the probability of the accident you just experienced, for others. You include your previous lack of awareness of these facts in your definition of how the accident got *on your board*. Or you might simply notice that you take a certain risk every time you step into a car.

Being the board is not about turning the blame on yourself. You would not say, "I should have been more aware of the loopholes in the laws . . ." or, "It's my fault I didn't look behind me when I stopped at the traffic light" or, "I know I brought this on myself." Those would be sentiments from that other game, the game in which you divide up fault and blame.

GAINING CONTROL VERSUS MAKING A DIFFERENCE

Because, in the world of measurement, we live in the illusion that we have only ourselves to rely on, our need for control is amplified. So, when mistakes are made, and the boat gets off course, we try to get back in control by assigning blame. The "shoulds" and "oughts" from the blame game give us the illusion that we can gain control over what just went wrong, and that's an illusion of language again. Of course we can't change it or control it—it has already happened!

The practice of *being the board*, is about *making a difference*. If, for instance, after hearing all your good ideas, your boss makes one mistake after another that you warned him about, you may think to yourself, "He never listens, he's competitive with me—he just wants to be right." And you feel once again like a prophet unsung in his own time or like Cassandra watching the towers of Ilium fall. This is a time you can use the practice of *being the board* to make a difference. Here is how you might proceed.

"*How did it get on the board that my boss is not listening to me?*" you ask yourself. Soon you notice that "not being listened to" has become an abstraction for you, with meanings attached, like: he doesn't *want* to listen to me, or he is competitive or closed-minded. You know full well that you have had many such experiences in your life or you would not have recognized this one coming down the road. So you say, "How would I describe what is happening if I were to take away those extra elements of my story?" And when you point to real things instead of abstractions, you boil it down to: "I told my boss what I thought and he did not take my advice." Now you can draw a conclusion that gives you leverage. You can say without fear of contradiction, "My boss did not take my advice because he was not enrolled in it. It is up to me to light the spark of possibility. So if I want to make a difference, I had better design a conversation that matters to him, one that addresses what and how he is thinking."

Whereas "should haves" are commonplace in the fault game, apologies are frequent when you name yourself as the board. That is because when you look deeply enough into the question, "How did that thing that I am having trouble with get on *the board that I am?*" you will find that at some point, in order to give yourself a feeling of control or equilibrium, you have sacrificed a relationship. Whether you got into silent combat with your boss because he did not take your advice, or you failed to speak truthfully to your daughter because you did not want to upset her, or you just did not recognize how important you are to an old friend; at some point, a relationship broke down or is in the process of breaking down. And your effectiveness has deteriorated with it. In these cases, an apology often serves as a restorative balm.

But in the model of fault and blame you cannot authentically apologize if you do not believe you are wrong, according to a shared measure of responsibility. It would be foolish for the pawn in the game of chess to apologize to the bishop for not having captured a piece five diagonal squares away, in a location where the rules prohibit him from moving. But when you, as the pawn, name yourself as the board, you can easily say to the bishop, "I think I sensed that you did not have a thorough knowledge of the rules, yet I failed to enlighten you. For that I apologize."

In the fault game your attention is focused on actions—what was done or not done by you or others. When you name yourself as *the board* your attention turns to repairing a breakdown in relationship. That is why apologies come so easily.

YOU MAY BE ASKING, "Why should I put so much emphasis on relationship when it will inevitably slow me down? Sometimes I just need to get a job done, and people have to understand that." Well, the answer is either they will or they won't. Sometimes you can enroll people in the necessity for short-term results, and sometimes your being heedless of the long line of relationship will slow down the overall "tempo" and run you into time-consuming difficulties.

CORA AND THE LONG LINE OF RELATIONSHIP

BEN: While the early days of rehearsing for a concert with a community or semiprofessional orchestra are easy-going, with the full performance only a light on the distant horizon, absenteeism is initially taken in stride. Members are juggling school, work, holidays, business trips, and conflicting performance obligations. But the final rehearsal days take on a more serious cast. For the Boston Philharmonic Orchestra, this cycle is amplified because of the rare position it occupies in the music world. The BPO maintains the essential nature and protracted rehearsal schedule of a community orchestra, yet it has gained a reputation for high-profile, high-quality live recordings and performances that are favorably compared with major professional orchestras whose fully recompensed players are required to attend every rehearsal. So, as the concert approaches, the pressure mounts, just as it would on an amateur baseball team about to play in the majors.

I was already anticipating a fraught situation before the Thursday night rehearsal for an upcoming performance of Stravinsky's ballet *Petrushka*. This was to be the penultimate rehearsal for a work considered by most musicians to be one of the most treacherous in its technical demands on both orchestra and conductor. The weekend's concert was being recorded live, with the intention of releasing it as the companion to a reissue of our CD of *The Rite of Spring*, a recording that had set a very high standard and had received much acclaim. Our performance of *Petrushka* was not going to go unnoticed!

Already, three student members of our viola section were going to have to miss the rehearsal because of a performing obligation with the Boston University Symphony Orchestra. A fourth had called in sick that afternoon. Only five violas remained, the very minimum to achieve any reasonable balance with the other sections.

As seven o'clock approached, I noticed that Cora, the assistant principal violist, appeared to be missing as well. One or two players seemed to think she had a chamber-music coaching session that evening. I was beside myself! Not only were we down yet another violist, but Cora had failed to notify either the personnel manager or me, so there had been no chance to persuade her to come or to find a substitute to sit in for the rehearsal.

I began working with the orchestra, my head turning continually toward the door, expecting Cora to walk in. How could she ignore such an important rehearsal? At the break, I rushed around the Conservatory looking for her, and finally found her on the third floor, chatting with two other students in one of the classrooms. I stormed in, saying (or was it shouting?) "Cora, don't you know that we have a rehearsal going on?"

Cora replied calmly, "But I told Lisa I wasn't coming tonight."

This made me even more furious. What was the use of her telling another member of the viola section, rather than the personnel manager or myself? And how could she be so nonchalant? "Cora, we cannot possibly do *Petrushka* this weekend with only four violas at the last rehearsal. At least come to the second half!"

"No," she said. "I have a coaching session tonight."

There was no coach in sight, and the young women did not even have their instruments unpacked. I said sarcastically, "Doesn't look like a coaching session to me!" and stormed off. I'm afraid I rather forgot *Rule Number 6.*

Cora arrived at the end of the rehearsal and said coldly, "I've decided to resign from the orchestra. I will not be abused like that."

Here was yet another problem thrust in my lap. "Oh, Cora, don't be silly," I said with irritation, "I wasn't abusing you; we're just under so much pressure because of the Stravinsky, and so many people missing."

She did not change her stance. "Well, I can't help that; that's your problem," she said and walked out.

Now I was really sunk. Our second best violist had just quit— no time to find a new one. That meant we were down to just eight violas for the all-important recording and concert. I went over it in my mind several times, thinking what could I do, what were my options?

As I frequently do on such occasions, I presented the problem to Roz and asked for her help. She said, "If you absolutely *have* to have Cora back in the orchestra for this concert, you have very little room to move. In that case you will have to persuade her to return, and since you are a master of persuasion, you don't need my help for that. If you are really angry and want a little revenge, you could even try to get her back for this one concert, and then fire her afterward." She smiled, testing me, but I was in no mood for humor. She went on, "But if you can imagine letting her go, you have some other options. Let me know if you decide that you are willing to consider playing the concert without her, and then we can talk it over."

At first, all I could feel was anger: "Why *should* I have to play the concert without Cora! She owes it to me to see this concert through!"—and then I clutched. "I can't get anyone else to play the Stravinsky, the performance is in only two days."

After a while I tried on the other scenario—eight violists, all who wanted to be there, all playing their hearts out. Wouldn't that be better than having a top-notch player whose injured attitude was pulling against the flow of the music? Now that I was no longer deeply submerged in the absolute necessity to have her back, I felt more open to hearing whatever Roz had to say.

"I can see that I don't absolutely need Cora, and I don't feel like persuading her or putting pressure on her to return," I told her. "I'm willing to risk that she won't come back. What, then, are my other options?"

And Roz said, "You can always grace yourself with responsibility for anything that happens in your life. You can always find *within yourself* the source of any problem you have."

"But that's ridiculous!" I protested. "I couldn't have stopped her from walking out, and anyway I have too many things to think about, I can't be responsible for everything every player does. I have a *concert* to prepare. . . ."

"Hold on," she said, "I'm not suggesting you blame yourself instead of Cora. This is a way of thinking that has nothing to do with *blame* at all." And she went on to explain the distinction.

I saw a completely new possibility and went to my desk to begin a letter. Cora had been a member of the Friday class, so she knew about the formulation of *giving an* A and writing a letter dated the following May. This was what I wrote to her:

October 6

Dear Cora,

I've decided to write you a letter like the one I asked each person in the Friday class to write to explain why they got an A this year. Here it is:

May 18

Dear Cora,

I got my A because I finally broke the cycle of lashing out at people when they didn't do exactly what I wanted them to do. I came to see that when I got angry with people or became sarcastic, it was like wiping them out, and our relationship never fully recovered.

It was hard for me to "get" that what I wanted was not necessarily what they wanted. For example, if we were preparing an important and difficult concert and players didn't come to a rehearsal or came late, I would be disappointed and angry because I thought that they should care as much about the project as I did and let nothing stand in the way of being there. Now I see that in a volunteer orchestra whose players have many other commitments, I cannot assume that everyone's priorities are exactly the same as mine.

I have come to realize that people will do what they want to do—which means that sometimes they will come to rehearsals and sometimes they won't—and I must respect their decisions. And if in my view they fail to adequately inform me of their intentions, I now ask them politely, to please, in the future, leave a message on the voice-mail, or inform the personnel manager directly, so that we can have some idea in advance of what to expect.

I see that conducting the BPO is an enormous privilege and that with it come certain risks: for instance, that I will not always have a full orchestra at important rehearsals. I know now that while I will do what I can to see that every chair is filled, I will accept the fact that this will not always be the case.

I have come finally to the realization that relationships with my colleagues, players, students, and friends are always more important than the project in which we are engaged; and that indeed, the very success of the project depends on those relationships being full of grace.

I have also realized that someone who stands up to me and is unwilling to accept abusive behavior is more of an ally than someone who goes along with it, either out of fear or resignation.

As a result of this breakthrough, I have a happier life, and so do the people with whom I interact. Even the music sounds better. So I think I really deserve the A.

Thank you, Cora, for being brave enough to guide me to this realization. I have known it for a while, but last night I really got it, that it is more important to make this breakthrough than to persuade, cajole, threaten, bribe, or charm you back into the orchestra. I have come to respect and appreciate you deeply. We will miss you.

Best Wishes,
Ben

People with whom I have shared this letter invariably ask me two questions. The first is, of course, "What did Cora do when she got the letter?" In one sense that question might mean, "Did your strategy work?" because after all we would prefer to get our way as well as have good relationships—we don't really want to have to choose between the two.

The answer is that she *did* return to her chair in the viola section, and I was thrilled; moreover, my relationship with Cora is now of a strong and enduring kind. This exercise truly took my attention off the issue of scarcity of time and players, which had me so often in a clutch, and heralded a different life for me. All sorts of situations that can be interpreted as crises of scarcity continually occur in the various orchestras I conduct, but now I recognize the specter of need and frustration as it appears. And I remember Cora. Once you have a new distinction, you have it forever. So, when people ask me the inevitable second question, "Couldn't that apology have been a manipulation, just another technique for getting Cora to do what you wanted her to do?"—the answer is yes, it could have been. You can take almost anything and turn it into a strategy. Yet, from the way I felt, the lightness and wholeness, my complete lack of attachment to the outcome—I know it wasn't.

JUST AS THE PAWN in the chess game is subject to the moves of the other pieces, white and black, much of one's life in the fault game is subject to others' actions, capacities, will, and whims. The perception of dependency arouses fear and leads to repeated breakdowns between us, which become the basis for the appearance of barriers and problems throughout life.

So, in everyday life, when bad things happen, we have a spectrum of response that includes guilt, blame, regret, helplessness or resignation, the sense of injustice, righteousness, and anger. But each of these responses actually takes us on a detour, into an eddy or a whirlpool, away from what we might call the living stream.

Let's see how it looks from opposites sides of the table when both parties practice *being the board*, requiring nothing of each other.

Two "100 Percents" Make a Whole

A man discovers his wife is having an affair and is devastated, because she did it and because she lied. In his pain, his response is to withdraw, get angry, blame, and reassess his choice of mate. She has changed; she is not the woman he knew. Everything seems different than before; he sits in the eddy trying to come to terms with the new reality, to get used to this new woman who was his wife, and to figure out what he should do. She has become the liar, the abuser, the stranger, and he struggles over whether he can and should treat her as someone he can talk to or whether she deserves to remain the enemy. He gets his friends on his side. Meanwhile things move ahead, and life passes him by.

If he were to adopt the practice of *being the board*, he would start by asking himself the question, "How did this get on *the board that I am?*" and if he is disciplined enough to stay in the game and not revert to the fault model, he will see something new that will empower him. If he looks long and deep enough, he will be able to tell the story with such understanding and, yes, compassion that a new world will open up for him.

Here is an example of what he might see:

This was the one thing that was not supposed to happen. He had made every attempt to let his wife know that infidelity was something he could not tolerate. And furthermore, they both agreed that honesty was the rock foundation of their relationship.

But, he asks himself, why was "betrayal" such an issue before it happened? Why had he made such a point of it?

He thinks of plenty of minor examples of betrayal in his life, starting as far back as when his mother left him at kindergarten in spite of his highly vocal objections. In fact, he realizes, one of the initial reasons he was attracted to the woman he married was that she seemed like a person who was not likely to oppose or betray him. She was accommodating and sensitive to his needs. He trusted her 100 percent.

When they fought, as he presumed all couples do, she accused him of not valuing her work. This was true—he realized—he was not really that interested in her marketing job. Yet he did his best to listen. They had agreed, he thought, that her desire to go to law school was probably unrealistic until they finished paying off his business loans; although he had said he would be willing to consider it at a future date. He felt that, by being a good provider and caretaker, he was all one could ask for in a husband.

In this moment of reflection, he noticed how resolute he had been in dismissing her independent experiences and desires.

His assumptions?

- Powerful, independent women betray.

- My wife is not one of those.

Does this mean that by ignoring things that were important to her he drove his wife to having an affair? That it was "his fault?" No, certainly not, and furthermore, it is not the game we are playing. Can he claim total responsibility for the breakdown that occurred in their relationship? Of course.

How might the same story look from his wife's point of view, if she were to adopt the practice of *being the board?*

Instead of justifying her actions by blaming him for not taking her seriously nor giving her the attention she deserved, she asks herself, "How did it happen on *the board that I am* that I did the very thing I promised—and really believed—I would never do?"

Perhaps she starts by acknowledging that she has never had an easy time balancing responsiveness and independence. Her formative years were riddled with guilt. Only when she had proven her loyalty and devotion to her mother, who had selfishly held on to her, had she felt free to live her own life. An assumption she lived by was that:

- Loving people support your independence.

She realizes she had not been able to contemplate that there might be a legitimate concern for the marriage in, for instance, her husband's resistance to her attending law school. She could only understand it as a kind of selfishness from which she had eventually to escape. She now realizes that between her total surrender to accommodating her husband and her growing need to escape, there had been little room for real partnership.

So, should she feel that the problem in the marriage was all "her fault?" No, that is not the game we are playing. Can she claim full responsibility for a breakdown in their partnership? Absolutely, as can he.

What can these two do? *She* could say to herself: "Of course he loves me. He deserves an apology; he's nothing like my mother." And *he* could say to himself: "When I look at it, it was absurd to hang on to her like a five-year-old and refuse to face that relationships grow and change. I had her in a vise grip. My first step is to apologize and see if there is anything left to build."

Together, they come up with new distinctions.

- Love is neither about self-determination nor sacrifice. It is a context in which two people build the life they want together.

- Strength and independence are qualities that can enhance a relationship.

In the practice of *being the board*, you are not concerned that the other person examine her own assumptions. You see that the "stumbling blocks" that stand in *your* way are part of you, not her, and only you can remove them. Moreover, once you embark on the practice, you may find yourself relinquishing your claim for "fairness" or "justice" in favor of the riches that an intimate relationship can offer.

WHEN YOU ARE *being the board*, you present no obstacles to others. You name yourself as the instrument to make all your relationships into effective partnerships. Imagine how profoundly trustworthy you would be to the people who work for you if they felt no problem could arise between you that you were not prepared to own. Imagine how much incentive they would have to cooperate if they knew they could count on you to clear the pathways for accomplishment.

This practice launches you on a soaring journey of transformation and development with others, a completely different route than the one of managing relationships to avoid conflict. It calls for courage and compassion. You do not find compassion simply by listening to people; you open the channel by removing the barriers to tenderness within *you*. Among the rewards are self-respect, connection of the deepest and most vital kind, and a straight road to making a difference.

CREATING
Frameworks

for Possibility

WHEN DR. MARTIN LUTHER KING, JR. gave his famous "I have a dream" speech to the crowd massed on the Mall in Washington, D.C., on that hot August day of 1963, he was addressing not only the thousands gathered there to hear him. He sought to awaken an underlying desire in all people: in the perpetrator and in the wronged, in whites and in blacks, the ones on this side of an issue and those on the other. King's vision spoke to that which is fundamental to any human being, the theme that unites and uplifts the people on the street, the privileged in the suburbs, and the politicians in office. He demonstrated with body and soul that dreaming can make a difference.

> We are simply seeking to bring into full realization the American dream—a dream yet unfulfilled. A dream of equality of opportunity, of privilege and property widely distributed; a dream of a land where men no longer argue that the color of a

man's skin determines the content of his character, the dream of a land where every man will respect the dignity and worth of human personality.

— DR. MARTIN LUTHER KING, JR.,
July 19, 1962

And he sustained the distinctions of that vision with his work and with his life.

The foremost challenge for leaders today, we suggest, is to maintain the clarity to stand confidently in the abundant universe of possibility, no matter how fierce the competition, no matter how stark the necessity to go for the short-term goal, no matter how fearful people are, and no matter how urgently the wolf may appear to howl at the door. It is to have the courage and persistence to distinguish the *downward spiral* from the radiant realm of possibility in the face of any challenge.

As a species we are exquisitely suited to thrive in an environment of threat where resources are scarce, but not always ready to reap the benefits of harmony, peace, and plenty. Our perceptual apparatus is structured to alert us to real and imagined dangers everywhere.

Yet we do have the capacity to override the hidden assumptions of peril that give us the world we see. We can open a window on a world where all is sound, our creative powers are formidable, and unseen threads connect us all. Leadership is a relationship that brings this possibility to others and to the world, from any chair, in any role. This kind of leader is not necessarily the strongest member of the pack—the one best suited to fend off the enemy and gather in resources—as our old definitions of leadership sometimes had it. The "leader of possibility" invigorates the lines of affiliation and compassion from person to person in the face of the tyranny of fear. Any one of us can exercise this kind of leadership, whether we stand in the position of CEO or employee, citizen or elected official, teacher or student, friend or lover.

This new leader carries the distinction that it is the framework of fear and scarcity, not scarcity itself, that promotes divisions between people. He asserts that we can create the conditions for the emergence of anything that is missing. We *are* living in the land of our dreams. This leader calls upon our passion rather than our fear. She is the relentless architect of the possibility that human beings can be.

But the gravitational pull of the *downward spiral* is strong indeed; it is the milieu in which we dwell. How do we reliably bring forth possibility in this context and take to our wings?

FRAMING POSSIBILITY: THE PRACTICE

The practice of this chapter is to invent and sustain frameworks that bring forth possibility. It is about restructuring meanings, creating visions, and establishing environments where possibility is spoken — where the buoyant force of possibility overcomes the pull of the *downward spiral*.

The steps to the practice of *framing possibility* are:

1. Make a new distinction in the realm of possibility: one that is a powerful substitute for the current framework of meaning that is generating the *downward spiral*.

2. Enter the territory. Embody the new distinction in such a way that it becomes the framework for life around you.

3. Keep distinguishing what is "on the track" and what is "off the track" of your framework for possibility.

Here is a story in which a leader creates a framework for the possibility of learning to live with differences. It tells how she ever-so-elegantly entered the territory.

A New Children's Story

A little girl in second grade underwent chemotherapy for leukemia. When she returned to school, she wore a scarf to hide the fact that she had lost all her hair. But some of the children pulled it off, and in their nervousness laughed and made fun of her. The little girl was mortified and that afternoon begged her mother not to make her go back to school. Her mother tried to encourage her, saying, "The other children will get used to it, and anyway your hair will grow in again soon."

The next morning, when their teacher walked in to class, all the children were sitting in their seats, some still tittering about the girl who had no hair, while she shrank into her chair. "Good morning, children," the teacher said, smiling warmly in her familiar way of greeting them. She took off her coat and scarf. Her head was completely shaved.

After that, a rash of children begged their parents to let them cut their hair. And when a child came to class with short hair, newly bobbed, all the children laughed merrily—not out of fear—but out of the joy of the game. And everybody's hair grew back at the same time.

THE TEACHER INTERVENED on the divisions occurring in her classroom by reframing the meaning of the child's strange appearance, releasing the little girl from her identity as a feared alien. The teacher distinguished baldness as possibility—a fashion statement, an act of choice, a game to play, an opportunity for solidarity and connection. No one was made wrong. There was nothing to fix. And the new statement was more compelling to the children than their fearful imaginings because it provided a whole field of play.

In the realm of possibility, there is no division between ideas and action, mind and body, dream and reality. Leaders who *become* their vision often seem uncommonly brave to the rest of us. Whether from the middle of the action, or from the sidelines, they are a conduit for carrying the vision forward. Like Gandhi or

Martin Luther King, Jr., they simply don't *resist* stepping into the breach with everything they have if they see that is what is called for.

> *Legend has it that an encounter took place between King Christ-*
> *ian X of Denmark and a Nazi officer shortly after the occupation*
> *of the Danish capital in April 1940. It is said that when the King*
> *looked out the window of the palace and saw the Nazi flag with*
> *its swastika flying over the roofs of the government buildings, he*
> *called for a meeting with the commander of the occupying forces.*
>
> *The King requested the flag be removed. The Nazi officer*
> *refused.*
>
> *King Christian walked a few feet away, and spent some*
> *moments in thought. He approached the officer once more.*
>
> *"And what will you do if I send a soldier to take it down?"*
>
> *"I will have him shot," the officer replied.*
>
> *"I don't believe you will," said the King quietly, "when you*
> *see the soldier I send."*
>
> *The officer demanded that the sovereign explain himself.*
>
> *King Christian said, "I will be the soldier."*
>
> *The flag came down within the day.*

THE THIRD STEP of our practice, distinguishing the on-track and off-track, is about maintaining the clarity of the framework. Being "off-track" often signifies that the possibility of a venture is momentarily absent, or forgotten, or has never been clearly articulated. Perhaps people have been riding on their initial feelings of inspiration, which have begun to fade. Sooner or later things tumble into the dualistic structures of right and wrong and spiral downward.

HIGH SPIRITS IN SÃO PAOLO

BEN: On our 1997 tour to Brazil, the New England Conservatory Youth Philharmonic gave its first big public concert in the Teatro

Municipal in São Paolo after three exhausting days of rehearsing, sightseeing, and touring. The house was filled to capacity. The enthusiasm of the warm-hearted, passionate Brazilian audience was overwhelming. Brazilian national television filmed the event and, afterward, projected it on a ten-foot screen in the foyer so the kids could see themselves. They were high as kites. Now the problem was to calm them so they could get to sleep and be fresh for the concert the following day. It was after midnight when we returned to the hotel.

The next morning I received an angry note from a guest saying he had been woken by a group of noisy musicians. Several other guests had been disturbed as well, the hotel staff informed us. Four students were found on the roof after 3 A.M., and four others were picked up in an unsavory part of town in the early hours of the morning by the security squad of our sponsor, BankBoston.

The next day, the orchestra was to play not one but two concerts, an outdoor event at 6 P.M. in front of fifteen thousand people, and an indoor performance at 9 P.M. of Mahler's technically and emotionally draining Fifth Symphony. The chaperones swung into action and demanded that I read the students the riot act. They wanted me to remind the kids that they had signed a contract prior to setting out on the tour forbidding them to consume alcohol or break curfew.

Roz and I consulted on the telephone, from Brazil to Boston, and addressed the problem, as we always do, with the question, "What distinction shall we make here that will bring possibility to the situation?" A broken contract points to the dualism of good and bad, and leads into the *downward spiral*, so we looked for another framework in which to consider the young people's behavior. I realized that while the rules for the tour had been carefully set up in contract form, I had never formally discussed with the kids their purpose for being in Brazil, beyond giving concerts. Purpose, commitment, and vision are distinctions that radiate possibility. We decided that I should hold a conversation about vision with the group, as a framework for addressing the late-night events.

Summoned to the auditorium, the diffident young players sat as far back as possible, their teenage bodies in various postures of exhaustion and protest. Every face, innocent or malfeasant, reflected that they were about to receive a well-deserved dressing down. "Last night after the concert," I began, "a woman came to me and told me with absolute honesty that the two hours she spent listening to Mahler's Fifth Symphony had been the most beautiful two hours of her entire life. You gave a great perform-ance last night, and she was not the only one moved and changed by it." Their faces looked blank for a moment, as though they could not hear these words that were so unexpected. After a pause, I went on, "What else did you come here to offer the Brazilian people?"

One by one, from various parts of the hall, came answers to the question: *We came to show them the best of America! That great music is a way of communicating friendship and love. We came to show respect for Brazil! That teenagers can make great music! That music can be fun! That we are happy to be here!* By now the answers were coming from all corners, and the faces were lit up with joy.

When exuberance and ease were palpable throughout the room, I said, "Of course, if you'd given a terrible concert last night, you probably would have all come home and gone straight to bed. It was precisely your exhilaration at having participated with so many people in great music-making that resulted in four kids being on the roof. It's just surprising that they didn't float any higher on sheer energy! But does waking the hotel guests at night represent the gift we wanted to bring the Brazilian people? Obvi-ously not. We got off track. You have to know where the track is to get back on, and you've all just expressed that beautifully."

Two of the kids volunteered to write letters of apology to those who had been disturbed at the hotel, and others thought of addi-tional ways to brighten our image with the people of São Paolo. No

one felt blamed or made wrong. We left the auditorium with everyone in high spirits, ready to give two invigorating concerts.

Just as I was leaving the hall, one of the chaperones said, "But
you didn't punish anybody!" And then he added as an after-
thought, "Though, I don't suppose they would be in the mood to
give another great Mahler performance if you had, and, really, I
don't think we will have to worry about them again."

A VISION IS A powerful framework to take the operations of an
organization of any size from the *downward spiral* into the arena of
possibility. Yet, while most organizations use the term "vision" lib-
erally, we have found that few have articulated a vision in such a
way that it serves that purpose.

VISIONLESS MISSION STATEMENTS

The term *mission statement* is often used interchangeably with the
word "vision" in business and political arenas but, by and large,
mission statements are expressions of competition and scarcity. A
mission statement characteristically draws a picture of the company's future, including its position in the marketplace, and desig-
nates the steps to fill out the design. That design is more often than
not some version of the aspiration to be Number One; by definition an exclusive—and excluding—objective. This kind of statement may motivate people competitively, but it does not provide a
guideline for all aspects of the company, nor does it inform people
as to its meaning and direction. There is no long line.

Example: "We are to be the preeminent supplier of the most
innovative technology in office design in America."

(Between the lines, a little voice from inside or outside the
company walls is crying, "What about me?")

(Another asks, "Why?" "What for?")

VISION

A *vision* has the impelling force of a long line of music. Mozart's soaring duet from *The Marriage of Figaro* lifted the prisoners' spirits high over prison walls in the film *The Shawshank Redemption.*

> *I have no idea to this day what those two Italian ladies were singing about. Truth is I don't want to know. Some things are best left unsaid. I like to think they were singing about something so beautiful it can't be expressed in words, and makes your heart ache because of it. I tell you those voices soared higher and farther than anybody in a gray place dares to dream. It was like some beautiful bird flapped into our drab little cage and made those walls dissolve away. And for the briefest of moments, every last man at Shawshank felt free.*

In this way, a vision releases us from the weight and confusion of local problems and concerns, and allows us to see the long clear line.

A *vision* becomes a framework for possibility when it meets certain criteria that distinguish it from the objectives of the *downward spiral.* Here are the criteria that enable a vision to stand in the universe of possibility:

- A vision articulates a possibility.

- A vision fulfills a desire fundamental to humankind, a desire with which *any* human being can resonate. It is an idea to which no one could logically respond, "What about me?"

- A vision makes no reference to morality or ethics, it is not about a right way of doing things. It cannot imply that anyone is wrong.

- A vision is stated as a picture for all time, using no numbers, measures, or comparatives. It contains no specifics of time, place, audience, or product.

- A vision is free-standing—it points neither to a rosier future, nor to a past in need of improvement. It gives over its bounty now. If the vision is "peace on earth," peace comes with its utterance. When "the possibility of ideas making a difference" is spoken, at that moment ideas *do* make a difference.

- A vision is a long line of possibility radiating outward. It invites infinite expression, development, and proliferation within its definitional framework.

- Speaking a vision transforms the speaker. For that moment the "real world" becomes a universe of possibility and the barriers to the realization of the vision disappear.

Vision-Led Goals and Objectives

Inside of the framework of a vision, goals and objectives spring from an outlook of abundance. A goal—even the goal "to be Number One in office design in America"—is invented as a game to play. Games call forth a different energy than the grim pursuit of goals in the *downward spiral*. They draw out the creativity and vitality of the players, without denying that the level at which they play may have something to do with whether the team qualifies for the next round. Under a vision, goals are treated as markers thrown out ahead to define the territory. If you miss the mark—"How fascinating!" Neither you nor the vision is compromised. In the pursuit of objectives under a vision, *playing* is relevant to the manifestation of the possibility, *winning* is not.

Examples of "Visions"

Here are some examples, from our interactions with organizations, of visions that meet the criteria of frameworks for possibility. An international food distribution company was inspired by "a vision of a world in ethical, sustainable partnership." A company that designs inexpensive home products found their expression in "the possibility of joy in the everyday," and a group of officers from the U.S. Army resonated to "the possibility of a world living in freedom."

> *Barbara Waugh, worldwide personnel manager of Hewlett-Packard Laboratories, spoke of the transformation that took place when HP's competition-driven mission statement was finally turned into a real vision. "I grew up thinking that change was cataclysmic," Waugh said, "and probably accompanied by music. The way we've done it here is to start slow and work small. At some point, it begins to multiply, and you get transformation — almost before you realize it."*
>
> *It happened during a meeting to plan a celebration of creativity at HP Labs. Laurie Mittelstadt, a materials engineer, posed a simple yet powerful question to the group:*
>
> *"Why aspire to be the best industrial lab in the world? Why not be the best lab for the world? In fact, why not say 'HP For the World?'"[1]*

> *The subtle shift of language tapped into a new reserve of energy. A senior engineer created a picture of what "For the World" meant to him. He took the now-famous photo of Bill Hewlett and David Packard, both of them staring into the garage where HP began, and superimposed a photo of the Earth taken from an Apollo spacecraft. Waugh's group turned that picture into a poster for an HP Labs Town Meeting. People from the rest of the company became so enthusiastic about the image that about fifty thousand of them bought the poster.*

A vision is an open invitation and an inspiration for people to create ideas and events that correlate with its definitional framework.

---

[1] Katherine Mieszkowski, "Change — Barbara Waugh," *Fast Company*, December 1998, 146.

"Tonal" Organizations

A vision can also be likened to the "tonality" of a company or group—the key in which the piece is written. Atonal music— music with no home key—never developed into a universal art form precisely because there is no sense of destination. How can you know where you are unless you have a point of reference? Music that explores only simple tonic and dominant harmonies is boring because there is no room for development. Or analogously, how inspiring is it to work for a company governed only and for- ever by its habitual way of doing things? Complexity, tension, and dissonance can give life to an organization as they can to music, but they do not present a coherent structure unless you can hear the home key, or connect to a vision. When a vision is leading an organization, it is instantly and steadily accessible to all members of the group. A vision is the organization's own *toes to nose*. It becomes the source of responsible, on-track participation.

THE BOUNTY OF VISION

BEN: Under the leadership of our vision "Passionate Music- Making Without Boundaries," the Boston Philharmonic Orches- tra has flourished in the last four years beyond all expectations. Our budget has tripled, and we are running comfortably in the black—a most unusual situation for a nonprofit classical music organization—yet we've never raised the price of our lowest priced tickets, and we give away any returns to homeless shelters. We take on the projects that come our way that express our vision, and we find a way to pay for them, so every aspect of the BPO, including the budget, is defined within a framework of possibility. The results? Recordings that are compared favorably with major profes- sional orchestras, programs and talks to get people who have never been to a classical music concert excited about music, a tradition of preconcert talks that are now drawing almost a full house, and an annual event where we team up with the phenomenal Louisiana Repertory Jazz Ensemble to put on a great concert and a huge party with wild dancing. And when we want to do something like take the orchestra, two choruses, two children's choirs, and eight soloists—four hundred musicians in all—to Carnegie Hall in New York City to do Mahler's Eighth Symphony, we find a way to do it.

When the office staff insisted on renting a storefront in a busy urban shopping area, I remember being puzzled as to why they were so adamant—since the majority of our business is conducted on the telephone and computers. But they knew. Passionate Music-Making Without Boundaries cannot be shut in. So now we have a BPO "storefront" with flowers in the window and a huge mural of an orchestra at play, and music radiating out onto the sidewalk. We have installed a bench there so people can sit and listen and eat their lunch. Our oft-sung vision energizes us to find new ways to extend the reach of music and guides us in all our decisions.

After one of my talks to an international group of young CEOs, in which I spoke at length about the practice of "being a contribution," the president of a Hong Kong company came to me and posed a question that has been asked many times by many others. He said, "I like very much *contribution*. But what about money? You have to make money!" My answer was that money has a way of showing up around *contribution* because money is one of the currencies through which people show they are enrolled in the possibility you are offering. That answer apparently was not enough for him. He rapidly countered, "But what about the stockholders?"

At this point his diminutive wife standing at his side gave him a firm jab to the ribs and said, "No, not the stockholders, the *children!*"—because it turned out the company produced the motor for a tiny children's car. In his concern for the stockholders, this CEO had forgotten that the company was formed around the idea of making a toy that children would love to play with. And, in fact, that distinction may never have been clearly articulated as a vision, so it was the more easily lost, and with it the framework of possibility it could have provided. At that, the man laughed what I like to call "cosmic laughter," because he got the whole thing in that moment—how absurd human beings are, and how magnificent.

OFTEN THE EXPERIENCE of a personal crisis or a failure will constitute a basis for the creation of a personal vision, which in turn becomes the framework for a life of possibility. Alice Kahana, an artist living in Houston, has a painful and vivid memory of her journey to Auschwitz as a fifteen-year-old girl. On the way, she became separated from her parents and found herself in charge of her little eight-year-old brother. When the boxcar arrived, she looked down and saw that the boy was missing a shoe. "Why are you so stupid!" she shouted at him, the way older sisters are inclined to do. "Can't you keep track of your things?" This was nothing out of the ordinary except that those were the last words that passed between them, for they were herded into different cars and she never saw him again.

Nearly half a century later, Alice Kahana is still living by a distinction that was conceived in that maelstrom. She vowed not to say anything that could not stand as the last thing she ever said. Is she 100 percent successful? We would have to presume not. But no matter: Such a distinction is not a standard to live up to, but a framework of possibility to live into.

ENVIRONMENTS FOR POSSIBILITY

The person who rigorously maintains the clarity to stand confidently in the abundant universe of possibility creates an environment around him generative of certain kinds of conversations. We come to trust that these places are dedicated to the notion that no one will be made wrong, people will not be talked about behind their backs, and there will be no division between "us" and "them." These environments produce astonishing results that can take people in wholly unexpected directions, perhaps because all their gates are open—inviting us to play in the meadows of the cooperative universe.

THE SKY IS NOT THE LIMIT

BEN: I often begin my Monday master class at Walnut Hill with a topic that has only tangential relationship to music. It is a way of getting the students to think of their lives in a wider context than the daily routine of practice, classes, and occasional performances. As a teacher I have an enormous opportunity to create possibility in every conversation. One class launched into a fascinating discussion about risk, danger, and breaking through barriers. Because I was going to NASA to give a leadership talk the next day, it occurred to me to ask the students to write about the similarities between the NASA program and their life with music. They know by now that what I mean is, "Talk about the dreams and aspirations in common, talk about spirit, talk about *being*." But I wasn't altogether prepared for the mastery with which they spoke of both music and the space program *as possibility*. Here are some of the spontaneous expressions they jotted down in class, addressed to the people I was about to meet at NASA.

> *In the same way NASA uses mathematics and machinery, we musicians must use sound. Sound can explore the soul, coax out dreams and possibilities that before were lost in inky blackness. A beautiful sonata escapes gravity. We are not very different, you and I. Our minute individual persons are small, but our life-journeys can span galaxies. NASA is granted billions of dollars and, for the insistence of possibility it bestows on the world, it is worth every penny.*
>
> *Amanda Burr, age 16*

You are the diplomats, the representatives of the world over here. You are going into the nowhere to search and to be intrigued at the smallest inkling of discovery. You are representing us to discover, explore, and find the possibility to escape the box known as earth, and go as far as possible. You have the responsibility to push thinking and ideas beyond limits, into the ethers, through the nothing into the something. . . . Music is similar to space, it is an exploration, a responsibility to push through the confines of pages of music, to go as far and as fast as the mind will work. . . .

Dave Lanstein, age 16

The world counts on you to open up new possibilities and discover what we humans can do. . . . The only time when music or space have boundaries is when humans create them. Thank you for keeping the possibilities alive.

Ashley Liberty, age 14

When I came to give my talk to the NASA employees at the Robert Goddard Space Center, I walked on stage, looked out over the sea of faces, and saw there the very people described in the letters I held in my hand. During my presentation I told the NASA audience about the young people at the Walnut Hill School, read the letters, and left the originals with them. Not long after, I received a communication from the project manager. He said that the presentation had had a big impact and had helped reenergize and refocus many in the audience who had forgotten why they had come to work for NASA in the first place. And then he went on:

NASA was . . . incredibly moved by the talented young students who wrote their wonderful "letters to NASA." The letters captured a simple beauty as to why NASA exists. The students communicated in a way that those of us who work here have never been able to express. As you know, each person asked for a copy

*of the letters and was overwhelmed by the power of the message
and the talent of your students.*

*Our people were so moved that they decided to write letters
to your class. Their enclosed letters are a personal "thank you"
and reveal a side of NASA not typically seen—a warm, emotional side that gets to the core of why we do what we do.*

*Please let your students know that when we showed the let-
ters to one of our Space Station senior managers, the decision
was made to include them on future space missions. The letters
will be placed on a CD-ROM being prepared for the initial
builders and inhabitants of the Space Station. Your students'
words will continue to inspire our explorers, especially during
the long and isolated times when they will face their greatest
challenges in space.*

*On behalf of all of us at NASA, please give our heartfelt
thanks to your students for their inspiration.*

Sincerely yours,
Ed Hoffman
Program Manager, Program/Project Management Initiative
National Aeronautics and Space Administration Headquarters

NASA did send a CD-ROM with the letters from the students
at Walnut Hill School into space. Their words and aspirations are
now circling the earth on the International Space Station.

And here are a few of the many letters the people at NASA sent
to the young people at the Walnut Hill School:

*Your comments about our efforts at NASA were very much
appreciated and very heart-warming to me. Often we hear
about the high cost of space flight but not very often the positive
aspects. The way that you pointed out the positive aspects
brought a tear to the eyes of many of us.*

*Thank you for reminding me of what I am here for. I will have
to remember "I am here today to cross the swamp, not to fight
all the alligators." Thanks.*

*Thank you for your beautiful and eloquent words of encourage-
ment on space exploration. They so poetically remind us of our
grander purpose. Coming from you, explorers of sounds and
keepers of the future, they are particularly meaningful. Each of
us, in our own way, works to evoke a greater depth of understanding of our past, present and future. May your sounds reach
the stars.*

THE PRACTICE OF framing possibility calls upon us to use our
minds in a manner that is counterintuitive: to think in terms of the
contexts that govern us rather than the evidence we see before our
eyes. It trains us to be alert to a new danger that threatens modern
life—the danger that unseen definitions, assumptions, and frameworks may be covertly chaining us to the *downward spiral* and
shaping the conditions we want to change.

But look what magical powers we have! We can make a conscious use of our way with words to define new frameworks for possibility that bring out the part of us that is most contributory, most
unencumbered, most open to participation. And why not say that
is *who we really are?*

Here is an example of a leader, *framing possibility*, offering a
new way for us to define ourselves. Nelson Mandela is reported to
have addressed these words of Marianne Williamson's to the world
at large.

Our deepest fear is not that we are inadequate,
Our deepest fear is that we are powerful beyond measure.
It is our light, not our darkness, that most frightens us.
We ask ourselves, who am I to be brilliant, gorgeous, talented,
    and fabulous—
Actually, who are you not to be?

You are a child of God.
Your playing small doesn't serve the world.
There is nothing enlightened about shrinking so that other
    people

Won't feel insecure around you.
We were born to make manifest the glory of God within us.
It is not just in some of us: it is in everyone,
And as we let our own light shine, we unconsciously
Give other people permission to do the same.[2]

---

[2] Marianne Williamson, *A Return to Love* (New York: HarperCollins, 1992). Formatting has been changed.

Telling the

WE Story

BEN: When I was nearing the end of my first sojourn in America on a limited visa, I set up a program that allowed me to take a group of American high school students back to England to study music for a year. Each of their high school principals in the United States had miraculously agreed to give them a full year's credit for the time spent there. I rented a house for them near Hampstead Heath in London, and instituted a complete course of study that included music, art, philosophy, and English. I arranged each week for a scholar to come to a dinner cooked by the students, to talk to them about his or her particular field.

On one occasion I invited my father, Walter Zander, who had devoted a lifetime to thinking and writing about conflict, especially the conflict between Jews and Arabs. By candlelight over a dinner into which the students had put extra care, he began by describing the whole sweep of Jewish history reaching back to the days of Abraham. He poured his passion into the tale—the great biblical stories, the medieval ages, the accomplishments in the arts and sciences, the story of the Diaspora and the tragedy of the Holocaust. He brought the whole saga down to rest on the tiny sliver of land called Palestine in 1947, the year before the land was partitioned between Arabs and Jews so that the Jews could have a homeland.

Then he went back and narrated the whole sweep of the history of the Arab people. He again started with Abraham, the acknowledged ancestor of the Arabs as well as of the Jews. He spoke of Arabic sciences and learning, the magnificent library at Alexandria, the great artistic achievements—the tapestries and the architecture, the music and the literature, the folkloric *Tales of the Arabian Nights*. Above all he spoke of the legendary courtesy of the Arab people.

What was most striking was that he seemed to speak with equal enthusiasm whether he was speaking about the Jews or the Arabs. When he brought the great four-thousand-year saga of the Arab people down to the same little sliver of land called Palestine in the year 1947, one of the students exclaimed, "What a wonderful opportunity! What a privilege for both those peoples to share that land and that history!"

Imagine if this sentiment had been the one to guide Arab and Jewish relations in the Middle East since 1947.

MORE OFTEN THAN NOT history is a record of conflict between an Us and a Them. We see this pattern expressed across a broad spectrum: nation to nation, among political parties, between labor and management, and in the most intimate realms of our lives. What framework will transform us AND those whose claims on resources, territory, and the "truth" are irreconcilable with ours? What can we invent that will take us from an entrenched posture of hostility to one of enthusiasm and deep regard?

To begin the inquiry, we have distinguished a new entity that personifies the "togetherness" of you and me and others. This entity, the WE, can be found among any two people, in any community or organization, and it can be thought of, in poetic terms, as a melody running through the people of the earth. It emerges in the way music emerges from individual notes when a phrase is played as one long line, in the way a landscape coalesces out of the multicolored strokes of an Impressionist painting when you get some distance, and in the way a "family" comes into being when a first child is born. The WE appears when, for the moment, we set aside the story of fear, competition, and struggle, and tell *its* story.

The WE story defines a human being in a specific way: It says we are our central selves seeking to contribute, naturally engaged, forever in a dance with each other. It points to relationship rather than to individuals, to communication patterns, gestures, and movement rather than to discrete objects and identities. It attests to the *in-between*. Like the particle-and-wave nature of light, the WE is both a living entity and a long line of development unfolding. This new being, the WE of us, comes into view as we look for it— the vital entity of our company, or community, or group of two. Then the protagonist of our story, the entity called WE, steps forward and takes on a life of its own.

By telling the WE story, an individual becomes a conduit for this new inclusive entity, wearing its eyes and ears, feeling its heart, thinking its thoughts, inquiring into what is best for US. This practice points the way to a kind of leadership based not on qualifications earned in the field of battle, but on the courage to speak on behalf of all people and for the long line of human possibility.

The steps to the WE practice are these:

1. Tell the WE story—the story of the unseen threads that connect us all, the story of possibility.

2. Listen and look for the emerging entity.

3. Ask: "What do WE want to have happen here?"
   "What's best for US?"—all of each of us, and all of all of us.
   "What's OUR next step?"

THE ALCHEMY OF WE

ROZ: One might think that a treatment facility for schizophrenic and autistic children would be as unlikely a setting as one could imagine for the WE to emerge, but it was there in the Master's Children's Center in New York City in the late 1960s where I first saw it clearly. One of my patients was a strange and poetic nine-year-old named Victoria Nash. At any moment this child might strike a pose and hold it for hours until someone recognized her gesture and interpreted the reference; for instance, "Oh, you are Giselle and you are feeling sad!" At the opening of this vignette, as so often, she was twirling on one foot.

"Go to the store!" she said, addressing me imperiously while gazing off into the distance. "Go to the store and get me what I want." I stifled a smile, and did proper homage to the solemn nature of the request. "Yes, your majesty," I replied, bowing. I left her in the room to wait for me and crossed the street to the little corner store. I was enjoying the game, particularly because I prided myself on my sensitivity in finding the right things for people. This would solidify our relationship, I thought, wearing my therapist hat and taking myself quite seriously. I perused the shelves. What would she want? Something to read? No. Something sweet? She wasn't a junk food sort of girl. A fat can of Dinty Moore Beef Stew arrested my eye, momentarily. Then my gaze roamed over the sodas and juices in the refrigerated section and returned to the canned foods. I selected the Dinty Moore.

In the room with the blue shag rug and the simple white curtains, Victoria stood poised, her head cocked, staring at the paper bag in my hand. Then all at once I realized, "I am at her mercy.

She is about to invent us; she has that power, and this is her game. This is not about me and my talent for choosing gifts; it isn't even about my purchase. This is about *US*." And I saw the whole thing, the story of human connection that had been unfolding while I had narrowed down my sights to matters of personal pride. I realized we were at a critical point in the narrative. She was going to declare who we were, whether we were together or miles apart. Courageously I faced her. Bravely she faced me back. She took the bag, opened it carefully, and extracted the can of Dinty Moore. "Oh, Miss Stone," she said, relief suffusing her face. "How did you know this is exactly what I wanted?"

Victoria chose to tell *OUR* story, the story of sufficiency and connection, yet she might, perhaps more easily, have told a story about *her* disappointment over *my* shortcomings. It is an ongoing choice for all of us—when a lover neglects to call, a colleague lets us down, or someone surpasses us, we can choose to tell the story of the WE or the story of the Other.

USUALLY WHAT WE MEAN by the pronoun "we" is "you-plus-I," and so the questions "What shall we do?" or "What will work for us?" generally refer to a compromise between what you want and what I want. The assumption is that people are singular, constant beings whose stated desires are for all time. So it follows that some will win and some will lose, and neither are likely to get all they want. The resulting competition structures us in two ways: It encourages us to exaggerate our positions and keep back some of the truth, and it pushes us into offensive and defensive positions, so that we are all too soon handing out ultimatums and guarding our turf.

The practice of the WE offers an approach to conflict based on a different premise. It assumes there are no fixed wants nor static desires, while everything each of us thinks and feels has a place in the dialogue.

Here are some examples contrasting the I/You approach and the WE approach:

The I/You approach:

He says, "Give me a raise or I'm quitting my job."

His employer passes the buck, or tries to appease him, or lies to him, or tries to get him to put off acting on his decision.

Compare this to the WE approach, in which the assumption is that the entity WE, the in-between, is forever evolving, forever in motion. Often just the use of the word *we* can shift the direction things takes.

The WE approach:

He says, "We're apparently both happy with my work, and I sense our loyalty is mutual. Yet this salary doesn't support the other commitments in my life. What do WE want to have happen here? How can WE make the whole thing work?"

Here is another I/You conversation:

She says, "Get that woman out of your life or I will leave this marriage."

He lies to her, or tries to appease her, or tries to get her to change her mind to give him more time.

And the WE approach:

She says, "I am miserable with this situation, and I believe you are too. I'm so angry I don't know what to do. And I love you. What do WE want to have happen here? What's best for US?"

The practice of the WE gives us a method for reclaiming "The Other" as one of us.

Traditional methods of resolving conflict, all the I/You approaches, tend to increase the level of discord because they attempt to satisfy the dichotomous positions people take, rather than providing the means for people to broaden their desires. I/You methods deprive people of the opportunity to *wish* inclusively. They do not give people the chance to want what the story of the WE says we are thirsting for: connecting to others through our dreams and visions.

While the WE practice can enhance any aspect of your life, it also poses a risk. It is not a technique for arriving at a decision based on known quantities; it's an integrative process that yields the next step. It asks you to trust that the evolution you set in motion will serve you over the long line. What happens after that is not in your control, but springs spontaneously from the WE itself.

THAT WHICH WAS LOST IS FOUND

ROZ: My sister and I became guarded with each other in the weeks and months after our mother died. I don't think either of us had a handle on what it was about, but I, in my characteristic way, was eager to roll up my sleeves and iron out some issues with her. She, less given to argument, preferred to keep her distance. Many is the time I drove through the streets of Boston presenting my case in the most cogent terms to a full courtroom just beyond the dashboard, while she was safely closeted a state away.

My birthday came and went and still we had not managed to get together; of course I felt all the more put upon. Finally I had the grace to ask myself, "What's happening here?" and I caught a glimpse of the *in-between.* All the energy I had been expending to shape a persuasive argument was actually propelling us apart. And I missed her—acutely. I thought that if I could just *see* her we surely could find some solutions. So I called her, and invited myself to her house for breakfast, and got up in the dark and was down in Connecticut by seven. There in the kitchen in her nightgown I found her, looking like my favorite sister in all the world.

We talked gaily while we drank black Italian coffee, and then we took a long morning walk down the leafy dirt roads of Ashford, Connecticut, while her chocolate Lab, Chloe, ran ahead and came back, ran ahead and came back, in long arcs of perpetual motion.

What did we talk about? The architecture, and the country-side, and the cats that Chloe was eager to visit at the farm ahead. We revisited scenes featuring our hilarious mother. We talked about my work, and about a paper she was about to present. My "case" never came up; it must have gotten lost somewhere along that wooded road because by the time I got in the car—my court-room, my favorable jury—it was no longer on the docket.

Did we resolve the issues? Obviously not, but the issues them-selves are rarely what they seem, no matter what pains are taken to verify the scoreboard. We walked together, moved our arms, became joyous in the sunlight, and breathed in the morning. At that moment there were no barriers between us. And from that place, I felt our differences could easily be spoken.

My disagreements with my sister were but blips on our screen compared to the hostilities individuals and nations are capable of when anger, fear, and the sense of injustice are allowed to develop unchecked. "Putting things aside" then becomes quite a different matter. At the apex of desperation and rage, we need a new inven-tion to see us through.

No Human Enemy

Just such a device was forged out of an unusual interaction with a couple in my psychotherapy practice, a couple on the verge of sep-aration. The husband, who had resisted coming to the session in the first place, had retreated to the farthest corner of the office, albeit only a few feet away. His wife was in a rage at him for his habit of withdrawing, just as he was doing then, and for leaving her alone too often. As the tension built, she pleaded with him and accused him and then she literally howled at him: "YOU DON'T LOVE ME!"

I heard my own voice shouting back at her "Who *could* love you when you act like this?" and realized that I had hurled myself between them. This was pretty terrifying for me—never mind what they must have felt. I was standing a foot from the woman's face, the face of someone with whom I had worked intimately and whom I knew very well, saying the most untherapeutic thing imaginable. I was truly out of the boat. In a split second of fear I made eye contact with her, and I suddenly caught sight of her *central self*.

"But it's not you speaking," I blurted out. "It is something else: Revenge. Revenge is speaking in your voice. It's a creature, sitting on your shoulder, and it's going to get him no matter what, even if it has to destroy you in the process." And the creature appeared, right there on her shoulder, in front of our collective mind's eye.

Suddenly and miraculously I wasn't angry and I wasn't trapped, and our sense of connection was completely restored. Moreover a whole new set of phenomena appeared. I saw how much harder it was on the woman to have to manage this Thing than it was on the rest of us. I saw the vicious circle in which she would have to blame her husband for her outrageous behavior just to keep her sanity, while the Revenge Creature celebrated its victory. It was clear to me that It had come into being and split off from her at some early age and had not evolved since then by an inch or an ounce. And, I knew it was all a metaphor.

The man moved out of his corner and stood by his wife. Things came into view, one after another. "It's not going to enjoy being discovered," I said. "It's scheming right now to find new hiding places so it can make use of you again to get him." The woman turned to her husband: "What she is saying is true. I hate being this way!" And he grasped it completely by the tone in her voice. She plaintively asked me how she could get rid of the Thing.

I felt confident in telling her she would not be able to do away with it, as though I were an expert on Revenge Creatures; but in fact, once it was distinguished, I knew exactly how it would behave. I knew that if she resisted, it would gain in strength, and if she brought it to the light of day, it would lose its power. "Just keep calling it by name," I told her, "assume it's lurking somewhere." Ask yourself, "What's the Creature doing now?"

Here was an apparition—part invention and part discovery—that removed the barriers between us and allowed for a flow of compassion, no matter how badly we had behaved. It meant that wholeheartedness between people was always possible. I saw that if we describe revenge, greed, pride, fear, and self-righteousness as the villains—and people as the hope—we will come together to create possibility. We don't have to restrict ourselves, and we don't have to compromise. With our inventive powers, we can be passionately for each other and for the whole living world around us. We need never name a *human being* as the enemy.

IN OUR WORLD, terrorism is one of the ultimate expressions of revenge, breaking down trust and community. How do we tell the WE story in the face of this seemingly inevitable process? How might the practice of the WE proceed in a community violated by the acts of terrorists?

The practitioner of the WE starts by generating, for himself, the WE story: that people are their central selves, that communities are always seeking to evolve toward integration, that the enemy to conquer is never a human being. He encourages the expression of each thing that is pressing to be said in the group, not as a problem that must be resolved, but as a statement that can take its place with others. He does this until all that wants to be said is spoken, until all of all of us shows up. He holds the framework for the long line, and keeps the question alive, "What's best for US?"

Many voices emerge:

"The terrorist bomber should die for his heinous crime."
                    "That's just more violence."
"He and all of his kind must be locked out of our community."
                "How can we ever recover?"
"How do we stop this from ever happening again?"
   "How do we compensate the families?"
                        "The anger has no end."
"Fear is gripping our community."
        "What about the children?"
            "How does this happen?"
            "What do we want to have happen here?"

And the WE story, through someone or through many, begins to take hold. When the WE voice speaks it may say, "If we want to increase the community's strength against inhuman forces, let's include the terrorist in the discussion, along with the families and the townspeople and the security forces and the government. Let's hear what he thinks about why this has happened and what can be done with him for the sake of the community. Because he is one of US.

SYM•PHON•'I•A

ROZ and BEN: At the generous invitation of a friend whom we met at the World Economic Forum in Davos, Switzerland, we visited South Africa in the summer of 1999 with Roz's daughter, Alexandra. Along with the stunning beauty of the landscape and the rich variety of life, we were struck by one very remarkable thing: conversations everywhere centered on South Africa. All the enormously stimulating discussions we had, with government ministers in Cape Town or with artists in Johannesburg, with business people in Pretoria or with music teachers in Soweto, all the discussions were about South Africa. Whether we talked with our driver, or the chairman of the board of the Cape Town Symphony, or the cook, or the washerwoman, we found ourselves talking about South Africa. South Africa, the embodiment of *symphonia*, the sounding of all the voices together. A living, breathing entity.

Returning from a visit to a medical clinic in the township of her name, Alexandra said: "What's so amazing is that nobody is hiding anything. All the problems of society hit you in the face. You can see the terrible conditions of the squatter camps, and the total disparity among people's lives. It's all in the open. And it is tolerable," she said, "because you see that it's not how people want it to be. It seems as though everyone knows that everybody is trying to change it. They don't identify a particular group as being a problem. It's the whole society that has the problem, like a broken bone. I wonder how much of this has to do with the work of the Truth and Reconciliation Commission."

TRUTH AND RECONCILIATION

Mandela's post-apartheid, fully representational South African government confronted the dilemma that faces every nation emerging from a long period of savage violence. What attitude do you take toward the perpetrators, the people whose very existence intensifies bitterness and hatred in an already wounded society? What policies do you adopt to heal the nation?

To address this question, the South African government put into place a framework for the possibility of the integration of all aspects of society, and appointed Archbishop Desmond Tutu as its chairman. The Truth and Reconciliation Commission (TRC) offered amnesty to individuals who were prepared to tell the whole truth, publicly, and could prove that their violent deeds had been politically motivated. If an individual chose not to appear before the Commission, he or she agreed to be tried in conventional ways. Written into the South African constitution was the vision of the TRC: "a need for understanding, but not for vengeance, a need for reparation but not for retaliation, a need for *ubuntu* [brotherhood] but not for victimization."[1]

It might seem that Mandela's government took a huge risk by instituting the Truth Commission. After all the atrocities, wouldn't justice have to be served? Might not people otherwise take the law in their own hands? But the TRC appears to have been founded on another story, the story that we really are our *central selves* longing to connect, seeking a structure that supports us to dissolve the barriers. It seems, too, to have been predicated on the idea that when the all of all of us is out in the open, and our capacity to be with *the way things are* expands, communities will naturally evolve toward integration. The Truth Commission served as a framework for possibility whose results, as is always the case, were unpredictable.

More "truth" was revealed than anyone had imagined was hidden, coming to light by degrees throughout the proceedings of the TRC. As one story after another emerged, the dualistic definitions of victims and perpetrators shifted and new patterns were formed, deeper understandings, and perhaps the fundamental sense of connection that we were seeing on our visit. It was not uncommon, apparently, to see the perpetrators break down in tears as they described their actions to the very families they had violated.

As a young woman realized, having just heard a policeman tell how he had killed her mother: "The TRC was never supposed to be about justice; it's about the truth."[2] The all of all of us. Designed to put the impulse for revenge at one remove and to bring forward the enemy as a human being, a part of US, it was a framework for the possibility of social transformation.

---

[1] Anthony Sampson, *Mandela: The Authorized Biography* (New York: Knopf, 1999), 521.

[2] Gillian Slovo, *Guardian*, 11 October 1998, quoted in Sampson, *Mandela*, 521.

And, as Mandela said, the Truth Commission "helped us to move away from the past to concentrate on the present and the future."[3] It left the society free to take the next step.

WHILE VISIONS GO IN and out of favor, the WE remains, holding our heartbeat, moving on the impulse of the long melodic line of human possibility. Transformation from the "I" to the WE is the last practice and the long line of this book: the intentional, ongoing dissolution of the barriers that divide us, so that we may be reshaped as a unique voice in the ever-evolving chorus of the WE. Each of us can practice it from any chair, every day, anywhere. The practice of the WE draws on all the other practices. And if you attune your ear, you will hear the voice of the WE singing through each one of them in harmony.

ROSARIO

BEN: The New England Conservatory Youth Philharmonic Orchestra was on tour in Chile, and it was a day in which we had a recording session in the afternoon and a concert in the evening. I thought it was better not to have a rehearsal in the morning as well, but I was also wary of how exhausted the young players might become if they were let loose on the town. So I gathered the entire orchestra, eighty-eight strong, in a large reception room on the top floor of the Carrera Hotel in Santiago. I asked them to bring their individual parts so that we could go through the music together. Instead of assuming the role of instructor, I invited them to comment about the performances we had been giving on the tour, especially questions of interpretation. They responded to the invitation magnificently, as though they had been waiting patiently for

---

[3] Sampson, *Mandela*, 524.

me to ask. They did not need me to conduct the session, they took it over themselves, and about half of them spoke up during the nearly three-hour session. They didn't confine their observations to things that related to their own parts: a trumpeter offered an insight about a viola passage, and a woodwind player discussed the tuba part as though he were about to perform it. I felt honored to be their conductor.

A couple of days later, we found ourselves on what was supposed to be a twelve-hour bus trip—but that stretched out, as a result of various mishaps, to be a seventeen-hour journey through Argentina. We had performed the night before in the world famous Teatro Communale in Santiago and were now making our way through Argentina to our engagement in the hallowed Teatro Colon in Buenos Aires, stopping off to give concerts in a couple of smaller towns along the way. Although no complaint was heard from any member of the orchestra during the lengthy bus ride, I was concerned that general fatigue would cause a perfunctory performance in the less-than-prestigious hall in the small town of Rosario.

Looking for a new way of rehearsing the by-now excessively familiar *New World* Symphony of Dvorak, I asked the orchestra to reseat itself on the stage, so that as many players as possible were placed next to an unfamiliar instrument. A first violinist stood next to the timpani, an oboe player amongst the violas, a horn in the cello section. One of the double bass players even put himself between the concertmistress and me. The purpose was to reveal new sounds and textures that the musicians could not hear from within their own sections.

In addition, as was our custom on each day of the tour, I read aloud a quotation to serve as a point of inquiry for the rehearsal. "Never a door closes, but another one opens" was the thought for the day. I asked the players to imagine they were completely blind. They began to play the Dvorak with eyes shut tight. After a few moments, I stopped them. It was clear to all of us that the special flexibility and freedom we had worked so hard over the many months to create had been lost, leaving only a square rigid beat that they clung to in the absence of a visible leader. "When the door of eyesight closes," I said, "what door is likely to open?" "Listening," was the immediate response from several members of the group. We started again.

I walked to the back of the hall as they played, and was astonished to find that a new kind of music-making was emerging in that rehearsal hall like a landscape revealed at last by the dawn. Eighty-eight musicians, none of whom had intentionally memorized the score, were playing not by memory, but by heart, the entire first movement of Dvorak's *New World*, with an elasticity of timing rare in an orchestra of seeing musicians, unfathomable in an orchestra of blind ones. I saw that several of the visitors in the hall, teachers and music students from Rosario, were weeping, moved as I was by the connections present on stage and in the hall, and by something like a new voice, a true one, audible for the first time.

Uplifted, I returned to the stage and asked the young players to imagine that they had miraculously recovered their eyesight and still found themselves on the shores of this New World of listening. As we performed the first movement of the Dvorak once more, all eyes fully open and ears tuned to the finest nuance, I had the experience, so often sought, of wholeness of spirit. There was no leader, and there were no ones being led. Harmony was present. It was a high point not only of the tour, but also of the year, and it took place in a small town between the major engagements, where nothing of importance was likely to happen.

I am done with great things and big plans, great institutions and big successes. I am for those tiny, invisible loving human forces that work from individual to individual, creeping through the crannies of the world like so many rootlets, or like the capillary oozing of water, yet which, if given time, will rend the hardest monuments of human pride.

—WILLIAM JAMES

Coda

YOU MAY HAVE come to this book looking for solutions to some very real problems, or you may have opened it as an idle traveler passing through. Before long you must have realized that the book had no intention of solving your problems, or even of letting you browse. It was interested in providing you with tools for your transformation.

From what to what? From a person who meets the challenges life serves up, to one who designs the stage on which her life plays out; from a single note to a long line, from partial to full expression, from the I to the WE.

How? By the same route that musicians take to get to Carnegie Hall—through practice. Choose the practices that express yourself; they will keep you in the boat. They will shape your voice as a unique contribution to us all. You can turn your attention away from the onslaught of circumstances and listen for the music of your being; then launch yourself as a long line into the world.

Over the course of our narrative you may have redrawn, somewhat, your picture of the world. Being an "adult" may now seem like quite a different matter. Perhaps it brings to mind the artist, a person like yourself who affirms that he is living in a story and takes his hand to the creation of his life. The adult as artist, a one-buttock dancer with the cooperative universe, a willing conduit for possibility.

Remember how we used to dream as children of the delicious freedom and power of being grown-up? And somehow the dream vanished along the way, and we were energized only here and there by a job well done, a spirited gathering, or an occasional week in the sun? Now that we know it's all invented, let's revise this story. Let's just say that somewhere along the journey we carried too much, or slipped too often, or heard too many voices in our head, and wandered off the track. The possibility we saw so clearly as children got lost in the *downward spiral*, and we forgot the promise of our birth.

How fascinating!

Look around. This day, these people in your life, a baby's cry, an upcoming meeting—suddenly they seem neither good nor bad. They shine forth brilliantly *as they are*. Awake restored! . . . to the dream revived.

Acknowledgments

ROZ: We hired Carol Lynn Alpert as our editor to help us work out a structure for the book and weave its many divers and unusual elements into a musical line. While Ben was out in the world, breathing life into the new practices with corporate managers, orchestras, and students, Carol Lynn joined me in the later stages of organizing and shaping the voices, stories, words, and commas. She brought leadership to the task, great intelligence, a fresh imagination, and a wonderful sense of fun. In addition, she opened my eyes and heart to a possibility of partnership that lay outside of the box I had been living in and, happily, I will never be the same.

Vikram Savkar's thoughtful approach to research was invaluable to us, as was his intelligence in discussing the text, and his knack for finding a needle in a haystack when tracking references.

WE EVOLVED OUR WORK from very different backgrounds. Ben's development as a musician, a gifted teacher, and, above all, an inspired communicator, was encouraged by his spirited, community-minded mother, Gretel Zander, who was reliably blind to barriers. It was she who, when her nine-year-old son's musical compositions were negatively critiqued by a local adjudicator, promptly sent them to England's leading composer, Benjamin Britten. It was initially thanks to her that Ben was then shepherded into extraordinary musical mentorships with Ben Britten, Imogen Holst, and the great Spanish cellist Gaspar Cassadó. When Walter Zander asked the Spanish maestro for a bill for Ben's cello lessons, Cassadó waved him aside, saying, "If I charged what I thought my lessons were worth, you could never afford it," and proceeded to teach Ben for five years without charging a penny. Ben has carried that spirit of generosity forward by mentoring and arranging scholarships for literally thousands of young people. And he uses music as a medium to bring possibility to thousands of others: corporate leaders, accountants, doctors, young children, and people like Sarah at the end of their lives. His engagement is always a two-way street—he is guided and fulfilled by seeing others catch the spark of possibility and take it into their lives. *These* are the people Ben acknowledges.

My transformational leanings were also sparked by my mother, Lucy Stone, a woman of vast imagination and literary gifts. While an English literature background predisposed me toward constructivist or narrative therapy before the terms were popular, thinkers and writers like Erving Goffman, master of contingency, and Peter Berger, with his *Social Construction of Reality*, captured my imagination and altered my worldview. A short film on the work of Humberto Maturana that I saw in the early 1980s permanently shifted my perspective on how we know what we know. My mentor in family systems therapy, Dr. David Kantor, brought a world of interactions to light that were at first invisible to me, and pointed to a new possibility of transforming identity.

The teachings of Landmark Education, Fernando Flores, and Contegrity are compatible with and complementary to the story of life we tell in this book. We especially acknowledge Landmark Education for its emphasis on the discipline and power of making distinctions to transform one's experience of the world.

We want to thank and acknowledge my daughter, Alexandra Bageris, for her support for the relational side of the project: for her dedication to the all of all of us, and to our voices being fully expressed; and my son, Evan Bageris, for his contribution to the development of the Rule Number Six chapter, including his knowledge of the literature on alternative ways of viewing the self.

We thank Juliet and Urs Gauchat for their warm support—emotional, intellectual, and culinary—over the years of the project, and for keeping us straight on all the aspects of relationship that had to be considered in finding the form for the book.

I thank my dear friend Anne Peretz for her total dedication to the fulfillment of the vision, which entailed forgoing our annual painting trips, as well as being an ear for every difficulty; and my lifelong friends Susan Moon and Judy Nathanson, who were compassionate and helpful readers for early drafts.

Valuable collaborators in the evolution of this book have been the people in my practice who have worked so unreservedly to develop themselves and their lives. I am obliged not to name them. Perhaps, in another era, entering into psychotherapy will be defined not as remediation for personal failure, but as an esteemed discipline for evolving one's ability to contribute.

Other key collaborators have been Kent Lineback, Michael Mostoller, John Decuevas, Antonia Rudenstine, Christopher Wilkins, Kira Ayers, and Jeremy Trelsted.

Some places in the wild must be named as supportive ecosystems for the book: the summer tent on the island of Vinalhaven, Maine, where I lived and worked, and the firehouse overlooking the harbor that Bodine Ames provided; the cabin in conservation land in Duxbury, Massachusetts—the pond, and the woods, and the people who went out of their way in their busiest times to supply water and power.

ENORMOUS APPRECIATION goes to executive editor Marjorie Williams and director Carol Franco, who came to us with spirit and laughter, and, together with their colleagues at the Harvard Business School Press, made the whole project an embodiment of the practices.

A Guide to the Stories

About the Authors

ROSAMUND STONE ZANDER is a philosopher, an executive coach, a family systems therapist, an artist, and a writer. She proposes a theory of human development that promotes creativity as an essential adult capacity. Ms. Zander has brought wisdom, humor, and enlightenment to leadership teams at corporations and government agencies, and has conducted workshops at the Aspen Institute, the British Civil Service, National Public Radio, and the World Economic Forum, among others. A native of Cambridge, Massachusetts, she has a B.A. from Swarthmore College, continued her studies at the Bank Street College of Education, and received her Masters of Social Science from Boston University. She has held positions as a child therapist at the celebrated Master's Children Center in New York City and as a supervisor and instructor in family therapy at the Kantor Family Institute in Cambridge, Massachusetts and the Family Center/Parenting Journey in Somerville, Massachusetts. She had her first one person painting exhibition in 1981

Ms. Zander's latest book, *Pathways to Possibility*, further deepens the transformational ideas introduced by the Zanders in their best-selling, *The Art of Possibility*.

BENJAMIN ZANDER has been the conductor of the Boston Philharmonic since its formation in 1979, and the conductor of the Boston Philharmonic Youth Orchestra since its formation in 2013.

He has appeared as a guest conductor with orchestras around the world, giving regular performances with the Philharmonia Orchestra of London, with whom he is recording the complete cycles of Beethoven and Mahler symphonies. He has received three Grammy award nominations for these recordings. He taught at the New England Conservatory in Boston for 45 years, and was the Artistic Director of the music program for young performing artists at the Walnut Hill School. Born in England, Zander began composing at age nine, studied under Benjamin Britten and Imogen Holst, and trained as a cellist in Italy and Germany with cello virtuoso Gaspar Cassadó. He received a degree from University College, London, and pursued postgraduate studies at Harvard and in New York on a Harkness Fellowship. Zander is a sought-after speaker to major organizations on leadership and creativity. In 1999, he received the Crystal Award at the World Economic Forum in Davos, Switzerland, for his outstanding contribution to cross-cultural understanding. He is the recipient of the United Nations "Caring Citizen of the Humanities Award."

Read on for a selection from
Rosamund Stone Zander's latest book . . .

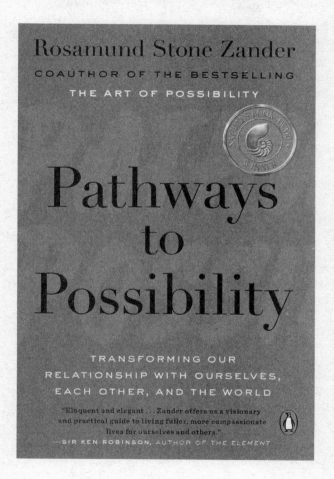

Introduction

If you do not change direction, you may end up where you are heading.

LAO TZU

IN THE DECADE AND a half since the publication of *The Art of Possibility*, its ideas and stories have evolved into something like a movement. People from multiple walks of life have taken up the practices and embedded them in their workplaces or in their family life. We get letters of gratitude from many with whom we have no connection—the producer who attributes the existence of the wonderful film *As It Is in Heaven* to reading *The Art Of Possibility*, a candidate for public office who whispers that he keeps it by his bedside as his guide. A company that was the only one in its industry that went cash positive in the 2007–9 downturn attributes its success to the concepts and messages in *The Art of Possibility*. We received a newspaper article in the mail that informed us that President Uribe of Colombia offered the book as his only gift to President Chávez of Venezuela in tense times, and we heard from many a parent grateful for being able to get on a more life-enhancing track with a son or daughter.

We cast out a pebble in a pond, and we are unable to see the

1

extent of the ripples although we know they go far. In those inter-
vening years, Ben and I, the authors of *The Art of Possibility*, haven't
stood still. Nor has the earth, for that matter. It has spun through
some sixty-three billion miles of space in the interim, sweeping up
new information from the universe and sending out its own messages. Meanwhile, Ben's activities have accelerated, as he has presented our model of Possibility to groups and institutions on every
continent. His astounding energy seems to gather its resonance
from the world around him, like fine crystal emitting harmonics at
the touch of a finger.

While Ben has been circling the globe, I have been doing a deep
dive into the inner world of our being, on a mission to discover how
we may continue to grow beyond what we settle for as maturity.
Most of us associate "growing up" with reaching a certain age, or
taking on responsibilities, or passing our wisdom and resources on
to the next generations. But I believe that when we become aware
of patterns in our behavior, when we learn to identify and rewrite
the stories that give us our identities, we will gain passage, at any
age, into a new phase of adulthood. In this territory of maturity,
where old fear-based patterns no longer hold us back, we will, I
wager, do what we now think of as remarkable, even magical, things.
In defiance of the adage "You Can't Change People," people around
us will change in our presence, step into productivity and contribution, and flourish. In this further phase of adulthood, we might well
be agents for powerful action in the collective interest, helping rain
forests to renew themselves, children to dedicate themselves to
worthwhile pursuits, and relationships between nations to thrive.
And further, when we become aware and adept at putting our out-
dated stories out of their misery and creating new ones, we have a
pretty good chance of experiencing that sense of profound and ecstatic connection to the universe that monks and shamans talk
about. It's to understanding and articulating this vision of human
growth and expansion that I have dedicated the last fifteen years.

The mission of *The Art of Possibility* was to teach people to distinguish two broad categories of approaches to life: one is the ev-

eryday attitude we call the "downward spiral," with all its joys and sorrows, triumphs and losses. The second approach we named "radiating possibility," and it is the attitude that life is a story we tell and live. The underlying assumption of the downward spiral is that life is all about survival, where you stand to win big if you are clever enough, get the right education, meet the right people, and make the best choices. But of course, chance and circumstances being what they are, in the downward spiral you are always faced with the fearful prospect that you might also lose. Your money may run out, the power you once enjoyed may disappear overnight, and the love you counted on may wane, or indeed be snatched away.

In the second approach, "radiating possibility," you can change your story at any time to be better adapted to the magnificent flow of the way things are, and the world will reflect the change in you, opening doors and showing you a path to where you want to go and what you want to do. This outlook gives rise to joy, love, and gratitude, leaving room for fear only in circumstances where feeling fear will mobilize you best to avoid an immediate threat to life and limb—a truck bearing down on you, for instance; not the prospect of losing someone's affection or being fired from your job.

So the first outlook, the downward spiral, is about the struggles over winning and losing, and the second, radiating possibility, is about creating the world in which you want to live. Each one is accompanied by its own distinctive postures, emotions, and expression. Each is a way of *being*. If, after spending time with *The Art of Possibility*, people were able to distinguish between the two attitudes through doing the practices, Ben and I felt we had accomplished our mission. At that point readers had a choice of perspective, and as a rule they chose to live in Possibility.

The current book, *Pathways to Possibility*, is firmly situated in the realm of possibility, but its mission is not focused on the distinction between the two attitudes addressed above. Your experience may deepen if you have read or choose to read *The Art of Possibility*, but it is not a necessary starting point for your journey through this manuscript. The mission of this book is to illuminate new pathways for growth. Throughout history, we human beings have bumped up against glass ceilings that have stopped us in our tracks and prevented us from going any farther, even in our imaginations. And then come the breakthroughs. Someone beats the record of the four-minute mile, and the door swings wide open for others. A black woman refuses to go to the back of the bus, and the whole of America wakes up, cheering or fighting, and from then on everything is different.

The glass ceiling I am addressing in this book is related to our assumptions of our limits as to how much we can grow and change, whether we can change others and even affect the world at large, and how much freedom and joy we can experience. To begin dismantling these assumptions, I trace how patterns we blindly enact get started and what we can do to initiate new ones, so that as we grow fearlessly and shatter the glass ceiling holding us down, others around us will grow as well.

The first part of the book attempts to demonstrate how the inevitable traumas of childhood provoke the young person into rigid patterns of thought and behavior that persist into the future. These childhood lessons such as "don't show when you are upset" or "dogs (all) bite" are designed to help us feel safe, but may be a poor fit, and may actually provoke danger, when carried into adult life. An example would be an instance where a friendly dog approaches a person who believes dogs bite. The man brandishes a stick, and soon there may be two frightened beings on the attack. The different stories in this section show how patterns develop and how they can be reengineered to reflect life as it is now and ourselves as we are now, in contrast to the environment in which they were first conceived, and our minds as we first conceived them.

The second part of the book turns our attention outward, and expands our vision to enable us to see through the individual stories and patterns that hold *other* people back. We learn to generate the combination of energy and love that is likely to enhance the possibility we see in others. Having rewritten our own stories in an adult voice, we avoid the common trap of being advice givers (at best) and meddlers (at worst) and we become natural agents for *their* transformation. We learn to connect with others on an energetic level that creates a synergy for realizing our collective dreams.

The third part shows how, having gained the capacity to witness our own patterns and contribute to an environment in which others can grow, we can become pioneers of a new territory where world and mind, mind and world are one. In this section you will read stories of remarkable accomplishments by people who sought to move in tune with the way things are, clear of wishful thinking and ideology, their minds open to patterns laced throughout our world; people who have gained a perspective on their place in it that allows them to enter into energetic connection with life around them.

The final section of the book presents a series of "games" that will usher the reader into this new territory of possibility and connection. These belong to the category author/philosopher James Carse dubbed "infinite games," open-ended engagements with no winners or losers; games that offer only the joyousness of play. The promise of this section is great: if we engage fully, we are likely to discover facets of reality we have never before experienced, and become occasional conduits for rare moments of perfect attunement with life.

You might think, from reading this introduction, that the book falls into neat compartments, but it isn't so. It develops in the way life evolves, in a radiating, spiral pattern that is anything but linear. So you will find you are experiencing echoes of earlier stories and ideas throughout the progress of the narrative, and this structure may help to give you a deeper perspective on each concept as it recurs in a different form. The possibility is that you will undergo an evolution of sorts, like a creature moving from the ocean onto land, that will leave you more aware of your primal beginnings but with greater capacities to move effectively in a new and expanded territory of life.

CHAPTER ONE

Voices, Ages, and Parts

I WORK BEST IN SILENCE in the wild. So I often write late into the fall on an island retreat, in Maine, when most visitors have already left to go back to the city. One particular day in October I walked down to the water and was looking out at the cove through a delicate screen of spruce branches. Lovely as the scene was—white sunlight on the water and all—I felt an unforeseen and quite unwelcome melancholy that sent my mind in three directions. One was to plan my escape from this troublesome sadness by leaving the island altogether and rejoining the busy world; I certainly couldn't be faulted for that; the season was well past. Another was to fret over the failings of my day, as in, "What have I actually accomplished?" And yet at the same time, I was noticing how lucky I was to be in this beautiful landscape. The emotional incongruity was not new to me, but this time it jolted me awake. Those melancholic feelings had belonged to my *mother*, I suddenly realized. They were only barely my own!

I remember, as a child, my mother speaking of bleak or gloomy feelings particularly in the summer, and such talk unsettled me. As I was her chosen confidante, I was the likely candidate to hear stories of the experiences that had disturbed her. Maine had been the place where her family gathered after a winter apart, but it was also an environment where she felt most keenly rejected by her older siblings. Later, when my grandmother died, my mother and her siblings had argued over the disposition of a family house that stood high above Penobscot Bay. As they were unable to agree, it was eventually sold—to my mother's regret. All of the members of that generation settled into summer houses of their own, but the tension between my mother and one of her sisters continued as an undercurrent whenever they were both in residence in that small community, until her sister passed away. Although Maine had meant privacy to my mother—a place of beauty and relaxation where she felt protected from the pressures of society—she wouldn't walk alone in the spruce woods for fear of the dark.

So even as I felt those twinges of sadness, I realized that while for my *mother* there were many disheartening memories associated with the trees and water, that was not true for me. I love the woods; I lived in a tent in the forest by the ocean for an entire summer by myself and was pretty much in ecstasy. So I surmised—as I stood there looking through the screen of dark spruces at the white sparkling water—that *something*, the slant of sunlight perhaps, or the sound of the bell buoy in the distance, put me in touch with a six- or seven-year-old part of myself that had absorbed my mother's feelings and her history. At that thought, a smile came over my face, the wisps of melancholy dispersed, and the landscape became once again the place I wholeheartedly enjoy. It occurred to me that in that little transformative awareness, I had redeemed us both, for notwithstanding moments of unhappiness, my mother had been inspirational in her love of the coastline, and that, too, had rubbed off on me.

"All of us, when we engage in relatedness, fall under the gravitational influence of another's emotional world, at the same time that we are bending his emotional mind with ours." I was struck by this passage in A *General Theory of Love*, by three neuroscientists, and had mused over what is really happening as we bring up our children, or share experiences with colleagues or friends. Are our minds covertly drawing their minds into attunement? Are theirs drawing ours?

Now looking out over the water, I asked myself, how is it possible that I can say "I feel sad" and a moment later I say, "No, it is not I that feels sad, but only a part of me that has absorbed my mother's sadness"? To what am I referring when I use the word "I"?

EMOTIONAL MASTERY: PART ONE

To shed some light on these questions and gain some mastery in the emotional arena, let's imagine for a moment that you and I comprise many different voices, ages, and identities. Picture that below your consciousness a host of characters have been busy making themselves comfortable in your psyche, like mice in the basement, heedless of how their presence fits with any business you are trying to conduct. Or imagine that these characters are like a family of invisible children that troop along with you to your employer's house for lunch, and just as you are making an important point, one of them upsets his water glass, or decides your boss is taking advantage of you and derails the deal.

And all the while you, like everyone else, take pride in being the master of your destiny. (The inner kids are having a good chuckle at that one.) Almost everyone, when confronted with some unpleasant piece of behavior he has performed that disturbs his sense of control, finds a way of justifying it, often by foisting the blame somewhere else.

"If you were more committed to me I wouldn't be so sullen."

"Sorry I haven't called—I've been deluged with work."

Sometimes those inner folks seem to be completely at odds with one another, as when with the best intentions to follow a course of discipline—a diet, say, or exercise regimen—you indulge. Or, you come dazzlingly close to someone and then you just disappear. Huh?

The best explanation for all this is that some parts of you, parts with the self-doubt or combativeness of a teenager, or even the confusion of a very young child, step forward and hijack the show. Then, predictably, they do it again, forming a pattern as distinctive as water in a riverbed.

Let's say that in frustration you complain to your friends, not for the first time, that a certain person is late for dinner, or doesn't call when he swore he would. They sigh and shake their heads over your inability to see the obvious: "That's just the way he is," they say. "You won't change him." No, that's not who he is, it's just one of his characters who keeps stepping up. But if you find yourself hoping that he won't do it again, well, that hope resides in a part of you, age five or seven or nine, who was impelled to trust someone who was patently unreliable, for your own survival's sake. That part of him and that part of you have minds of their own—they are not under his or your conscious control—and given certain circumstances, are bound like clockwork to come to the fore.

Each "part" of us appears to have a point of view about how life should go and is living a story of its own. Some of the stories grow out of the rubble of a traumatic situation where, as children, we perceive a life-threatening danger and figure out what to do about it. The story and patterns initiated in these instances we will call "safety patterns."

Other stories may get their impetus from the necessity to distinguish oneself in the sibling group, to get enough attention from the parents. It almost never happens that two children born consecutively into a family pop up with the same personality and identical interests. Each seems to know intuitively that he cannot bask in the very spot in the sunlight of parental attention that his sibling occupies and develops a unique way of being: what we call personality.

Personality is a major story for human beings, a narrative that gets defined and polished as time goes on.

Finally, some of our stories are shaped through daily exposure to the surrounding culture, beginning with the family. It's the story a person is "living into" that we notice when we identify someone as of a certain class, or as liberal or conservative, or as hailing from a certain country, or perhaps as our type or not our type. Our own stories are mixed in there as well, of course.

In the ensuing chapters you will see, through personal accounts, how individual stories are acquired and transformed. You will begin to understand how to find and articulate the physical, emotional, and cognitive patterns that are currently governing you, and you will learn to see them from the perspective of their author, yourself at a younger age, so that you will be able to rewrite them.

We begin our voyage with a trauma-based story in which we witness how a safety pattern was born out of a series of interactions that created fear in a child and overwhelmed his capacities. You may not always find this young hero of ours sympathetic, and that's intentional—desirable even. I want you to stay at an interested and neutral distance from which you can view Alan as he grows and perhaps find some aspects of yourself in him to consider with the same dispassion. My intention is to help to strengthen the observing part of you that really is your most valuable tool for making any changes.

So we open with the tale of this young boy, Alan, a child of divorce, who remembers the excitement of his father arriving from afar on Christmas Eve when he was three and a half.